T0179941

HUMAN-CENTERED LEADERSHIP
in Healthcare

Praises for
HUMAN-CENTERED LEADERSHIP
in Healthcare

"Human-Centered Leadership in Healthcare is one of those books that sets a new path in our thinking about leadership. This work looks at the person of the leader in an entirely different light. Using emerging knowledge related to complex adaptive systems and human-centered leadership practices, the authors have given us powerful insights and great tools for truly sustainable leadership going forward. This is a "must read" for anyone eager to embrace effective leadership for the future."

—**Tim Porter-O'Grady**, DM, EdD, APRN, FAAN, FACCWS
Senior Partner, Health Systems, TPOG Associates, Tucson, AZ.
Clinical Professor, Dean's Advisory Board, SON,
Emory University, Atlanta GA.

"Human-Centered Leadership in Healthcare is an inspiring and thought-provoking read for all healthcare professionals, especially nurses. The authors offer unique insight into the idea that all nurses are leaders, whether formal or informal, and that successful outcomes-driven leadership requires care for self, as well as care for other caregivers and patients. Through the introduction of the Human-Centered Leadership model, the text challenges readers to consider the type of leader they are, and the type of leader they want to be. By way of example and explanation, the model's inside-out approach to leadership is certain to resonate with nurses and others who have dedicated their lives to the service of caregiving."

—**K. Kelly Hancock**, DNP, RN, NE-BC, FAAN,
Chief Caregiver Officer, Cleveland Clinic

"There is no more important time than now to develop a human-centered leadership approach. Our complex pandemic world has left us all a little off balance. The authors of *Human-Centered Leadership in Healthcare* provide a path to find personal balance and leadership success by offering a guided journey to leading yourself and your teams in building a culture of excellence, trust and caring."

—**Nicole Gruebling**, DNP, RN, NEA-BC

"I have spent my entire career in healthcare focused on Human-Centered Leadership. It's the cornerstone of everything I believe in. This book does a beautiful job of giving nurse leaders all the tools they need to make Human-Centered Leadership a reality, at a time when they really need it. *Human-Centered Leadership in Healthcare* is filled with compelling evidence, great stories and most importantly great tactics to take your nursing leaders to the next level. And if you get nurse leadership right, everything else falls into place."

—**Quint Studer**, Author, *Hardwiring Excellence*
& The Calling: Why Healthcare is So Special

"Our recent experience with the pandemic has served as a crucial reminder of how vital human-centered leadership is to sustain a resilient healthcare workforce. In the book, *Human-Centered Leadership in Healthcare,* the authors present a roadmap on embracing self-care practices, developing authenticity, practicing courageous leadership, and building work cultures of inclusiveness and respect. The most complex person you will ever lead is yourself. Use the wisdom in this book to become the leader you are meant to be."

—**Rose O. Sherman**, EdD, RN, NEA-BC, FAAN
Professor Emeritus, Florida Atlantic University
Editor in Chief, Nurse Leader

"*Human-Centered Leadership in Healthcare* is the epitome of what we are craving as individuals, workgroups, and as a society—excellence, trust, and caring. Whether it be in government or healthcare or any industry in between, there's room for Human-Centered Leadership. The model calls for authenticity—in leaders and cultures—and establishes its foundation in evidence-based truths. With solid footing, it then not only gives its audience permission, but sets the expectation, that creativity, growth, and innovation are no longer what the few, elite organizations do, but are requirements for any organization's health and survival. The new normal for most of us will continue to be fraught with both environmental and human complexities and challenges. Human-Centered Leadership is a timely and essential investment in leaders—in any position and organizational cultures—in any industry."

—**Traci Thibodeaux**, MHA, CPME,
Chief Executive Officer, Beauregard Health System

"From the opening motto 'It starts with you, but it is not about you,' the reader is drawn into this important contribution to nursing leadership theory, Human-Centered Leadership in Healthcare. The concept that leadership cannot happen without a leader's deep understanding of self will resonate with new as well as seasoned nursing leaders. The authors present their ideas in clear and conversational dialogue that makes one feel as if they are sitting down with other nurses having a lively discussion about ways to improve how we practice and lead. The layout of the chapters is thoughtful and moves one from well-referenced concepts and clear clinical examples to discussion, then reflection, and on to proactive steps to apply the concepts. There are also important integration tables of the book's key ideas with innovation concepts, Magnet, ANA Code of Ethics, and the soon to be released AACN new competencies for nursing education. *Human-Centered Leadership in Healthcare* will make a major contribution to the nursing leadership literature and will be a welcome resource for practicing nurses, nurse leaders, and those in academia."

—**Margie Hamilton Sipe**, DNP, RN, NEA-BC, FNAP, FAONL
Director, Doctor of Nursing Practice program; Associate Professor
MGH Institute of Health Professions

"As a CNO and past president of the American Organization for Nursing Leadership, I believe Kay, Lucy, and Susan have written a compelling must-read book for anyone in nursing leadership or aspiring to be a nurse leader. The most important competency of a nurse leader is relationship management including communication. *Human-Centered Leadership in Healthcare* provides a practical approach to the nurse leader's focus on self and others. I recommend not just reading but sharing this book with colleagues as it is filled with great insights into nursing leadership."

— **Bob Dent**, Chief Nursing Officer, Emory Healthcare,
past president AONL, and author of 4 books including *Building a Culture of Ownership in Healthcare* and *The Heart of a Nurse Leader*

"*Human-Centered Leadership in Healthcare* is the product of a leadership journey taken by its authors who started out with a question regarding one's humanity and led to an important revelation. The ability of nurse leaders to truly and completely care for, develop, and connect with self and then others will result in a form of exceptional leadership achievable for those willing to learn how. Human-Centered leadership in nursing will transform you personally and professionally beyond your expectations, enabling you to do the same for others. Through this blueprint, these authors will guide you on how to enact this kind of leadership which is truly needed in today's healthcare landscape."

—**Laura Caramanica**, PhD RN CNE CENP FACHE FAAN
Professor in Nursing
Tanner Health System school of Nursing
University of West Georgia

To lead is to understand one's power, passion, and purpose in being a multiplier for individual and collective impact as an authentic and humbled leader. The intersection of leadership, love, service, and humanity is where *Human-Centered Leadership* originates and reflects the graciousness of those called to care and those called to support during the most sacred of acts — caring for others.

—**Cole Edmonson**, DNP, RN, FACHE, NEA-BC, FAONL, FNAP, FAAN
Chief Experience and Clinical Officer, AMN Healthcare

HUMAN-CENTERED
LEADERSHIP
in Healthcare

Evolution of a
R∃vo⅃ution

Kay Kennedy, Lucy Leclerc,
and Susan Campis

NEW YORK

LONDON • NASHVILLE • MELBOURNE • VANCOUVER

HUMAN-CENTERED LEADERSHIP in Healthcare
Evolution of a Revolution

© 2022 Kay Kennedy, Lucy Leclerc, *and* Susan Campis

All rights reserved. No portion of this book may be reproduced, stored in a retrieval system, or transmitted in any form or by any means—electronic, mechanical, photocopy, recording, scanning, or other—except for brief quotations in critical reviews or articles, without the prior written permission of the publisher.

Published in New York, New York, by Morgan James Publishing. Morgan James is a trademark of Morgan James, LLC. www.MorganJamesPublishing.com

Morgan James BOGO™

A **FREE** ebook edition is available for you or a friend with the purchase of this print book.

CLEARLY SIGN YOUR NAME ABOVE

Instructions to claim your free ebook edition:
1. Visit MorganJamesBOGO.com
2. Sign your name CLEARLY in the space above
3. Complete the form and submit a photo of this entire page
4. You or your friend can download the ebook to your preferred device

ISBN 978-1-63195-553-2 paperback
ISBN 978-1-63195-554-9 ebook
Library of Congress Control Number:
2021904059

Cover Design by:
Rachel Lopez
www.r2cdesign.com

Morgan James PUBLISHING

Builds

with...

Habitat for Humanity®
Peninsula and
Greater Williamsburg

Morgan James is a proud partner of Habitat for Humanity Peninsula and Greater Williamsburg. Partners in building since 2006.

Get involved today! Visit
MorganJamesPublishing.com/giving-back

For all nurse leaders. It's time to change the world.

Table of Contents

Acknowledgments

Transforming ideas, experiences, and research into a book is as challenging as it sounds. Those closest to us, our partners in this beautiful journey called life, provided us the space and encouragement to give voice to the nurse leaders we and others would follow to the end of the earth. John, Louis, and Mark deserve kudos, thanks, and redemption of quite a few IOU's for uninterrupted dinners.

Also, having a seasoned and world-renowned nurse leader like Tim Porter-O'Grady not just listen to our ideas but encourage, advise, and mentor through the genesis of Human-Centered Leadership is a gift to not just us, but to our profession. Words will fall short of the gratitude we have for the time and investment Tim has shown us. Thank you.

Finally, we want to give a big shout out to the Morgan James Publishing team for their creativity, encouragement, and support for believing in us and in our work.

Foreword

So many books have been written, and so many theories have been put forth on leadership—especially in the nursing field. However, to have expert nursing scholars share their vision, grounded research, emerging theory, experience and deep wisdom about leadership, from within, is a unique gift to this pressing and haunting human phenomenon. You will see in this work; it is all about humanity and all about you and NOT about you. It is about a higher consciousness that holds and captures the core truths of leadership as a universal living phenomenon of knowing/being/becoming a Human-Centered Leader.

Leadership is and cannot be otherwise—Human-Centered. That is all ye know and all ye need to know—with a Catch. The Catch—how to live it out—intellectually, experientially, evidentially, and currently, within and without—in complex and turbulent times with unspeakable challenges, that transcend self, system, society, in any field of practice.

This is where Kennedy, Leclerc, and Campis have gathered up their career experiences, their grounded scholarship, evidence, and deep, wise insights, of living leadership, to offer another way forward. This work is a welcome sanctuary, a breath of fresh knowledge, informing moral, passionate action, in this often-mindless field of strategies, tactics, formula, and endless platitudes that end up stale, over-used, and dead-ended.

Original and refreshing concepts and evocations invite the reader into this new/old leadership territory—opening up energizing guidance to awaken the human heart and mind. Concepts and language incite and elicit heart and head knowledge to sustain leader and leadership in right relation with Source; offering up ancient and perennial knowledge and knowing, that transcends time and space and unites a coherent model, theory, template, format, guide to deep transformation within and without. This is done so, playfully, embracing for example, "Two Tigers, A Mouse, and a Strawberry" as an inspired passage to mindfulness-in-action. Other playful truisms such as "It is Not about you"; "Trust—The Connector", and other universal timeless teachings expand and elevate our consciousness.

The authors challenge us to break set, through engaging innovatively in the imaginative "Power of thinking differently," combined with realities for facing the complexity of our chaotic world—opening space and heart for new possibilities of what might be, rather than conforming to what is.

When all is said and done, this leadership text is original, timely, wise and worrisome, in that it challenges a mindset that conforms to what has been, and no longer works; while simultaneously, pointing toward a new path and passage of leadership that transcends the past and also transcends disciplines. It offers universal insights, grounded evidentiary wisdom, and directions for a new, human-paced and human-faced road to leadership, not yet paved, but awaiting the next generation and next leader. It could be YOU.

—**Jean Watson**, PhD, RN, AHN-BC, FAAN, LL (AAN)
Founder/Director Watson Caring Science Institute
Distinguished Professor/Dean Emerita University of Colorado Denver, CON
jean@watsoncaringscience.org
www.watsoncaringscience.org

Preface

Most nurse leaders choose leadership because they want to make a difference, even while knowing that leading people poses one of the most challenging roles in healthcare. Leadership requires elevating, inspiring, and rallying people to use their skills and talents in order to obtain desired outcomes. As healthcare becomes more and more complex, effective leadership becomes more multidimensional. Most leaders accept that their role requires long hours and sacrifice and will include both successes and failures. In some cases, working yourself to exhaustion is seen as a "badge of honor" and practicing self-care, for many leaders, becomes a low priority. As we all know, exhaustion coupled with a lack of self-care leads to burnout and chronic stress. So the question becomes, what attributes must a leader embrace to be successful and resilient in both their professional and personal lives?

While meeting together over coffee, we three nurse leaders, all with years of nursing experience from the bedside to the boardroom found ourselves sharing stories about our lives and our careers. Our discussion began to move into the territory of leadership. We shared thoughts on modern leadership theories. We talked about respected nursing leaders and about the leaders we'd had during our careers—leaders we would follow to the end of the earth, as well as the leaders who made us want to resign from our positions, effective immediately. We finally began to discuss ourselves as leaders. We talked about our strengths, and we shared our "opportunities for growth." Woven through our stories were memorable moments of joy and success, and moments when we made a difference in others' lives, led teams to achieve difficult goals, published meaningful and relevant research, and even created culture changes. These stories also revealed symptoms of burnout, self-neglect, negative self-talk, and exhaustion. While most leaders don't often talk about this part of nursing, on this particular day, we did. In many ways, sharing our stories with each other and showing ourselves to be vulnerable and imperfect human begins became a cathartic and healing experience for us. We realized we had experienced many of the same emotions and a lot of the same frustrations.

We continued to meet for coffee each week, and over time, we decided to use our knowledge and experience to assist other nurse leaders, especially those who are new to the nurse leader role. We believe in order to be the best leader, one who creates a culture of excellence, trust, and caring, the leader needs to focus from the "inside out." Self-awareness, self-care, self-compassion, and mindfulness, now more than ever, need to become a part of the nurse leader's daily practice. The Human-Centered Leader understands that as healthcare becomes increasingly uncertain, complex, and ambiguous, the leader needs to be at the center, and by embracing self-care practices, authenticity, courage, inclusiveness, and respect for others, the leadership attributes of the Awakener, the Connector, and the Upholder will become apparent. We believe that the Human-Centered Leader will bear this motto in mind: "It starts with you, but it's not about you."

A Few Words About This Book

This is a work created to ignite bold and passionate nurse leaders from the bedside to the boardroom in reclaiming the essence of nursing as a human-centered profession. The structure of this book is designed to challenge your current paradigms of "good" and effective leadership in today's complex and challenging 21st-century world. The content is structured to present Human-Centered Leadership in Healthcare, as an evidence-based nursing leadership theory and approach, which we explore in Part I. Employing that foundational research, in Part II you'll start to work with the most neglected part of most leaders: yourself. Self-care, self-compassion, self-awareness, and mindfulness become the mantra and "fight song" of the Human-Centered Leader. You'll learn to stand up for your own well-being so you can then healthily emanate energy outward to others. In alignment with the theory itself, Part III guides you to become familiar with the three primary dimensions of a Human-Centered Leader: the Awakener, the Connector, and the Upholder. Each chapter includes exemplars, stories, and the voices of our research participants in order to translate concepts into real-world behaviors and ways of being. In Part IV, we devote a good bit of space to sharing ways in which you can strengthen the attributes of a Human-Centered Leader in your own practices. We refer to these "nuts and bolts" as techniques for developing the people who lead the people. Finally, the book concludes with an invitation to join the movement and transform Human-Centered Leadership into a revolution in nursing leadership. The call to action is authentic. We believe you'll recognize yourself somewhere in this book. We also believe you might just recognize that nurse leader you would follow to the end of the earth.

Voice. A brief note about the voice used in this book. While there are clearly three authors, the manuscript is represented as the collective voice of one. Our research and this book are infused with the voice of nursing. You'll find instances when we share stories from a personal, "I" perspective. These stories come from either our own experiences or have been garnered from experiences shared by colleagues over the past 30 years. Stories from this personal perspective are the greatest connectors, and we believe you'll find something familiar in many of them. Rest assured, names and minor details have been altered to ensure anonymity in both the positive and not-so-positive anecdotes. All scholarly or evidence-based information is cited to give credit to the appropriate author or source. We also used the collective "we" when aiming to share the united voice of the authors. The goal is to prevent you from wondering which one of the authors wrote this or that. Instead, we want you to visualize the writing as the voice of nursing.

Audience. The book is designed for a wide audience in nursing and healthcare. We envision utlity in book clubs for practice settings, such as shared governance councils or the chief nursing officer's executive team. Practice settings could also use this book as a foundation for leadership programs, especially those on a journey to excellence. We also see this text as a viable option for nursing programs from BSN to MSN to DNP. With mindful intention, we aligned the AACN 2020 *Draft Essentials Domain 10 on Personal, Professional, and Leadership Development* with the evidence-based attributes of the Human-Centered Leader. We provide a crosswalk of Domain 10 competencies for each attribute of the Awakener, the Connector, and the Upholder. We see this as an upstream effort to influence the leaders of tomorrow with a nursing-centric and human-centered way of leading. Finally, we created thought-provoking Reflection prompts to be used in either practice, or academica, as well as discussion questions for each chapter. The Reflections are aimed at individuals while the Discussion Questions are designed for just that, igniting groups to talk, to innovate, and to consider alternative ways of being. These are the keys to activating the learning in each chapter. Each chapter also includes a list of cited references as well as recommended reading to further engage thought and expand horizons of learning.

PART I
A NEW MODEL OF LEADERSHIP—
IT'S COMPLEX

Human-Centered Leadership in Healthcare embodies the principles of complexity science. It's different from traditional leadership in that the leader is embedded in the system. The influencers and innovators are those at the point of care. The Human-Centered Leader embraces change and unpredictability, knowing that it sparks innovation and progress. We share the highlights of the qualitative research findings that support the Human-Centered Leadership in Healthcare model as a grounded theory. The leadership model is introduced along with the guiding principle: It starts with you, but it's not about you!

Chapter 1

Recognizing Humanity in a Complex World

"Invisible threads are the strongest ties."
—**Friedrich Nietzsche**, Philosopher, Poet, and Writer

As I walk past a construction site for a new 600+ bed hospital in the middle of downtown, I pause to take it all in. The physical structure—steel beams, concrete foundation, and floor after floor where humans will be cared for during, quite possibly, the most vulnerable time of their lives—would soon be covered in complex mechanical, electrical, and plumbing systems. The building looks almost as complex as the humans who will fill it. Patients, families, nurses, providers, food service workers, housekeeping attendants, respiratory therapists, case managers, information technologists, plant facilities staff, security officers, volunteers, imaging technicians, medical records administrators—the list could go on for quite a while. The juxtaposition of this skeleton of hard yet resilient materials with the future occupants' fragile yet complex and resilient ways of being is quite a concept to consider. With so many systems and departments and diverse humans interacting within one physical space, who provides oversight and ensures it's all systems go? Who gets the honor of ensuring the patients and the teams caring for those patients have the resources, processes, and culture to be successful? Healing and caring for patients from birth to death requires not just team members, but leaders who remain focused on the humanity of those entrusted to their care.

Human-Centered Leadership is a contemporary approach, some will call it a movement, that aims to emphasize the importance of recognizing that leaders are as human as their teams and patients. *Human-Centered Leadership in Healthcare* embodies the principles of complexity science, just like the complexity of the systems in the shiny new hospital. Human-Centered Leadership is different from traditional leadership in that leaders are embedded in the system, working on every unit within the building. Traditional leaders are usually placed outside or above the system in the penthouse suite. In contrast, Human-Centered Leaders are recognized as nurses at the bedside as well as those who serve in the board room. The influencers and innovators are those at the point of care. So, what does point of care mean? It means that whatever role you play in the care of humans, you're charged with leading. This can mean you, as the nurse, lead the patient's care through coordination and connection of services from providers, respiratory therapists, physical therapists, and dieticians. It means you lead by being present with the patients and their families in a way that exemplifies your values and the values of your organization. It means you, as the nurse manager, create an environment that upholds and recognizes the humanity of your team members while awakening the excellence that exists in each of them. You build a community that creates a safe space for your nurses, giving weight to the importance of making their environment the best it can be, in addition to the environment of the patient. Think about your current role or a place you've worked in the past. Who were the leaders you'd follow to the end of the earth? What was it about them that made you feel that way? Who were the leaders who've made you leave, or consider leaving, a job? What was it about them that made you feel that way? Some aspects might come to mind quickly for both the "end of the earth" leaders as well as the "you make me want to quit" leaders. Often, the qualities of a leader are described in key words that label *how* a person leads, but their leadership might more accurately be described as a combination of things, ones that are often invisible or intangible. As we journey through the details of what a Human-Centered Leader is, we'll challenge you to consider great leaders and not-so-great leaders from your past, and most importantly, your own leadership approach, through several lenses: Starting with Self, Awakening, Connecting, and Upholding.

The Intent

Earlier we invited you to visualize the physical architecture and infrastructure of one hospital. When that hospital is finished, the steel beams and concrete foundation will, in effect, disappear from our direct sight. The solid structure holding up that building is now an invisible architecture. The beams are still there providing support, but we don't always have them at the top of our minds. They're always there, 24 hours a day, 7 days a week, 365 days of the year. They do their jobs and do them well. The hospital stands tall, stays cool and welcoming in the summer and toasty warm in the winter. We also invited you to consider the human architecture within that building. Nurses, doctors, and the whole team. Who makes up the biggest part of the healthcare workforce? In the hospital that's being built, I would put money on the fact that registered nurses (RNs) will be one of the biggest pools of human labor. Let's move outward a bit and consider the city's hospitals, clinics, home health agencies, and long-term care facilities. Well, why not think even bigger? What about the nation? Nurses are more than four million strong in the United States. Nurses are the invisible architecture that show up and care for humans 24 hours a day, 7 days a week, 365 days a year, year after year. Sound familiar? Just like the physical structure that holds up the building to meet its purpose in sheltering and comfortably housing humans who require care, nurses do the same for the humans entrusted to their care. The intention of this book is to share a new, yet familiar, way of leading that will resonate with nurses and, we expect, with all disciplines of healthcare professionals who have humans at the center of their purpose. As we consider this strong sense of purpose and commitment to care for others, the Human-Centered Leadership approach will assist you in putting a name to the qualities and attributes of that leader you would follow to the end of the earth. Hopefully, that's the leader you want to be. The primary tenets of Human-Centered Leadership will help you to identify how effective leaders start with self and then organically emanate their influential energy outward to their teams and to their patients. The book will walk you through a series of steps to identify and recognize Human-Centered Leadership attributes that already exist within your leadership style and will challenge you to consider how to strengthen other Human-Centered Leadership attributes that might not be as evident to you. You will be challenged to do a good bit of self-reflection and self-examination because, as we say in Human-Centered Leadership, "It starts with you, but it's not about you."

Why does Human-Centered Leadership target healthcare leaders and, specifically, nurse leaders? Remember, nurse leaders are defined as those from the bedside to the boardroom and all roles in between. To answer the question, Human-Centered Leadership was not intended to "target" a certain population; rather, the theory and approach emerged through a research process designed to be constructivist. This means, we asked nurses about their leadership experiences. Experiences as leaders and experiences being led by others. We asked them the same questions we asked you earlier. Who are the leaders you'd follow to the end of the earth? And who are the leaders who've made you want to leave a job? We weren't sure what we'd find but were happily surprised to discover a common tribe and humanity-centered way of leading existed within those "end of the earth" nursing leaders. Through the research process, which we'll describe in the following chapter, we put a name to something we all knew existed. Something that had not been named before but had been experienced repeatedly across all types of healthcare organizations and specialties. The primary intention of this book is to share with you that theory and a contemporary approach. The hope is you'll feel as if you're connecting with an old friend, that leader you knew years ago when you were a new nurse, or that leader you now work alongside. We also hope you'll recognize yourself.

INTENTIONS
- Discover and explore a contemporary leadership approach that exemplifies the essence of nursing.

- Illustrate how the attributes and behaviors of the Human-Centered Leader can result in industry-leading outcomes.
- Recommend practical approaches to maximize each attribute of the Human-Centered Leader at all levels of professional nursing practice: Self, Awakener, Connector, and Upholder
- Offer strategies to align attributes of the Human-Centered Leader at all levels of nursing education (BSN, MSN, and DNP) with the proposed *AACN Domain 10: Personal, Professional, and Leadership Development* (AACN, 2020)

DISCUSSION QUESTIONS

Think about a movement or revolution, such as civil rights or women's rights. Consider the awareness and change it brought. Today's world looks and behaves so differently due to the courage of everyday humans who paved the way. Those on the front line were bold. They took action to create a new way of being. In your opinion, do you believe nursing is stuck in the "borrowed way of leading" or the "way we've always done it"? Are we ready for a revolutionary paradigm shift to lead in a different way?

What's one way you can be part of a movement to lead in a different way, a way that would inspire your team to "follow you to the end of the earth"?

REFLECTION

As you consider the invisible architecture within your organization and the quote from Nietzsche at the start of this chapter, think about those leaders who represent "the strongest ties." What are the characteristics of those leaders?

_____

_____

_____

_____

REFERENCES

American Association of Colleges of Nursing. (2020). *DRAFT Essentials Domains, Descriptors,* Contextual Statements, and Competencies. https://www.aacnnursing.org/About-AACN/AACN-Governance/Committees-and-Task-Forces/Essentials

RECOMMENDED READING

Tye, J., & Dent, B. (2017). *Building a culture of ownership in healthcare: The invisible architecture of core values, attitude, and self-empowerment.* Sigma Theta Tau International.

Chapter 2

Show Me the Evidence

"Research is to see what everybody else has seen,
and to think what nobody else has thought."
—**Albert Szent-Györgyi**, Hungarian Biochemist and
1937 Nobel Prize Winner in Physiology or Medicine

I n healthcare, we deal in "best practices" and demand evidence to support the care of patients and our communities. We would expect a patient who arrives in the emergency department with symptoms of a stroke to be cared for in a way that reflects decades of evidence. From the time that patient arrives, the clock starts and a list of time-sensitive actions on the part of the providers and nurses is put into play. Brain imaging, IV access, STAT labs, NIHSS exams, 12-Lead ECGs, oxygen saturation and vital signs, administration of tPA Alteplase—and that's just in the emergency department! The evidence-based care continues throughout the patient's stay and long after discharge to home or rehabilitation. In fact, the evidence in that stroke patient's care lasts a lifetime. According to Han et al. (2015), when evidence is used by the healthcare team of registered nurses and providers, the patients are more likely to survive and avoid readmission during the subsequent 30 days. Think about that. Receiving specialized and evidence-based care provided by skilled human resources increases the likelihood that stroke patients will not only survive the initial episode but will also go on to recover successfully! This is an example of connecting evidence to outcomes, and in a theoretical sense, we're connecting a set of ideas and concepts to measurable results. What if we looked at leadership in a similar way? Which leadership approach do you subscribe to? Is it based in evidence? Is it specific to healthcare? Has it been proven to improve measurable outcomes, such as a healthy work environment, patient satisfaction, retention of staff, and reduced errors, or improved just culture? No need to answer right now. You'll have plenty of opportunities to consider these questions as we navigate the foundation of Human-Centered Leadership and its basis in evidence. Human-Centered Leadership in Healthcare is a theory and, we believe, a movement that will transform the culture within a hospital or clinic or community. What follows is an overview of the research we performed over a period of years to develop and define qualities of the leaders we would follow to the end of the earth. These are leaders who embrace a unique approach, recognizing humanity in each of their team members while, get this, caring for themselves first. Yes, what a revolutionary concept. We will also share how some of those leaders, including those of us writing this book, identified as servant leaders but soon discovered the burnout that comes with being focused on others all the time. The expense paid is health, well-being, and the ability to lead effectively for a sustained amount of time. Bear with us as we dip our toes in the worlds of theory and research. Keep in mind that those stroke protocols that save lives started with theories and research.

The Wind

Remember the Nietzsche quote at the start of Chapter 1 about invisible threads being the strongest ties? Think about that building downtown. The strongest ties might just be the people, not the steel beams. Keep reading. Stay with us. Let's start with the wind. The wind is a phenomenon we can't see or hold in our hands, yet we know it exists. It can be cold, hard, and biting as it moves over our face in the winter, or it can be warm, slow, and filled with grains of sand when we're at the beach. The wind can carry seeds to cultivate growth in new areas, or it can swirl into a wave of destruction as part of a hurricane or tornado. The wind is a concept so familiar to us, yet it is essentially invisible until characterized by what it carries or how it feels on our body. The wind is also influenced by its relationship with the environment as much as it influences the environment. The complexity of the wind's relationships is heralded by multiple weather models and theories.

In nursing, leadership models are like the wind. We can't hold them or see them. They're complex systems reflecting the interconnectedness of relationships, processes, and entities: all things we can't see or hold in our hands. Theories make phenomena and their relationships visible in a way one could only sense beforehand. Just as the temperature of the cold wind tells us the wind exists, theories come to life when we put words and ideas into a structure or map showing what we previously only sensed. Theories are made up of words and constructs to describe concepts with no physical referents. Within nursing, leadership models remind us of the wind, with complex relationships influenced by unique environments. Nursing has historically borrowed theories from the business world to explain leadership styles. Nurses describe themselves as "transformational" or "servant" leaders, to name just two. Why has nursing not explored the wind we all know exists? The invisible, yet "known," unique way of leading we've sensed for decades? We're not sure of the answer to that question, but we believe we've discovered a potential way of being you'll find familiar and effective.

The Research Journey

The phenomenon of nursing leadership is a social process rooted in human interactions. Nursing leadership lives and breathes within complex micro and macro systems. The unique nature of how nurse leaders effectively lead has not been well documented or researched in the literature. While much research and writing have been done on other forms of leadership, such as traditional, servant, and transformational, there remains a gap in the literature to document the approach experienced by many nurses and nurse leaders. When we first embarked on our journey to reveal that familiar "wind" of effective nurse leaders in our past, we discovered that nursing leadership research and publications employed borrowed theories in lieu of developing a unique theory or philosophy that clearly defines and explains the experiences of nurse leaders. We searched for evidence, narratives, or studies that described nurse leaders who skillfully merge metric success while recognizing the humanity in those receiving care, as well as in the caregivers (Porter-O'Grady & Malloch, 2018; Weberg & Fuller, 2019). The purpose of our research was to explore and explain how nurses and nurse leaders respond to and navigate the landscape of caring for complex humans within an industry confronted by high-stakes pressure to be efficient, lean, and profitable. In the spirit of our approach, rooted in constructivist grounded theory (more to come on that!), our guiding questions were simple and to the point: *How would you describe the nurse leader you would follow to the end of the earth?* and *How would you describe the nurse leader who made you consider leaving your job?* We wanted to see, hear, and understand the shared experiences and shared attributes of nurse leaders because nursing and healthcare deal with humans, not widgets or products shipped overnight.

In doing our due diligence to review the literature, we were surprised by the number of borrowed business theories used in healthcare. The results of our search revealed distinct themes regarding the most commonly employed models within nursing and healthcare leadership, which are notably borrowed from other disciplines: traditional, servant, and transformational. An exhaustive literature search revealed one proposed nursing-specific leadership theory based on a nursing practice theory—dynamic leader-follower relationship model (Laurent, 2000)—and one nursing leadership conceptual model—person-centered leadership (Cardiff et al., 2018). As a perspective check, we'll review the most commonly used leadership models within healthcare and nursing as a means to identify the gap in nursing-specific models and theories for leaders within complex healthcare systems. From this unique starting point—the historical evidence of borrowed theories applied to nursing leadership—we were able to study inductively the more specific experiences of nurse leaders.

Traditional leadership is also commonly referred to as "linear," "bureaucratic," or "transactional," and is typically understood to be top-down. The leader is at the top of the structure, and the followers or workers are employed to accomplish the goals set forth by the leader. Remember the building? Traditional leaders tend to stay cordoned off from the point of service. Porter-O'Grady and Malloch (2018) describe traditional leadership thinking as vertically oriented, hierarchical, mechanistic, reductionistic, compartmental, and controlling. Traditional leadership is generally authoritative and transactional, with minimal or no input from the workers at the point of service, which may suppress innovation and ownership in the work (Weiss et al., 2019). A traditional leader expects unit and organizational outcomes to result from the leader's authority or from their influence over the workers at the point of service, thereby controlling the environment and improving expected outcomes. Traditional leadership styles tend to focus on efficiency, quantity, and restricting the autonomy of team members in sharing innovation and ideas. The results of this approach are often mixed, with high output and achievement of goals but also low morale and limited trust among team members (Crowell, 2016; Weiss et al., 2019)

The transformational leadership model was established in 1978 by James McGregor Burns, a political scientist and noted scholar in leadership studies (Marquis & Huston, 2017). Extending Burns' work, Bass (1985) introduced transformational leadership theory and used the word "transformational" in place of "transforming." Bass developed a questionnaire with four components of transformational leadership: 1) idealized influence, 2) inspirational motivation, 3) intellectual stimulation, and 4) individualized consideration. Transformational leadership has been used effectively in diverse sectors including the military, education, organized religion, and human services. The hallmark of a transformational leader is someone adept at casting a shared vision that allows followers to invest and engage in actions, creating momentum toward the common vision (Lin et al., 2019; Weiss et al., 2019). Professional nursing has embraced the use of transformational leadership, and it is one of the five key components of the American Nurses Credentialing Center (ANCC) Magnet Recognition Program for establishing Magnet status in nursing care (ANCC, 2015). The effective transformational leader focuses less on managing change and more on the strategy around aligning followers with organizational goals and metrics (ANCC, 2015; Lanaj et al., 2016; Weiss et al., 2019). While much research has examined the effects of transformational leadership on those being led and on the organization, Lin et al. (2019) explored the effects of transformational leader behaviors on leaders themselves. They discovered the "dark side" of transformational leadership structured as a one-way street of influence and energy to cast and deliver on a vision which results in increased emotional exhaustion, burnout, and turnover among leaders.

Servant leadership is one of the more commonly borrowed theories or philosophies of leadership embraced within healthcare and nursing (Hall, 2015; O'Brien, 2011). Servant leadership is defined as an understanding and practice of leadership that places the good of those led over the self-interests of the leader. Servant leaders place the needs of others before their own and embrace a fundamental motivation to serve (Greenleaf, 1977; O'Brien, 2011). Servant leadership characteristics are rooted in altruistic motivation with emphasis on the characteristics of empathy, awareness, persuasion, foresight, stewardship, and commitment to supporting professional growth among team members and to active listening (Greenleaf, 1977). Since many in healthcare identify with this general approach, we wanted to learn more about the foundational evidence supporting servant leadership as an effective way of leading in healthcare. We found a rigorous report that identified the positive aspects alongside the deficits of servant leadership. Parris and Peachey (2013) completed a systematic literature review of servant leadership in organizational contexts across 39 research studies and found no consensus on the definition of servant leadership and no consensus on how its success is measured. Positive findings indicated servant leadership is considered a viable leadership theory that helps organizations improve the well-being of those being led. The potential challenges of systemic use of servant leadership in healthcare lie in a lack of evidence-based and standardized definitions as well as connections to metrics such as quality, safety, and patient satisfaction. Also, servant leaders have a tendency toward expedited burnout, and they are more likely to contemplate leaving a place of employment. Both of these effects derive from the sheer pressure of sustaining an exclusively others-oriented way of leading. Servant leadership remains untested in a systematically empirical way, supported only by a plethora of narratives and anecdotal literature that have not researched the basic constructs and relationship to outcomes (Parris & Peachy, 2013).

Nursing-specific theories for ***practice*** are prevalent however nursing-specific ***leadership*** theories are a rare find. Laurent (2000) conceptualized differences between management and leadership theory and proposed a leadership theory utilizing Ida J. Orlando's model for nursing. Laurent's model of dynamic *leader-followers* builds on Orlando's (1961) model for *practice* with proposed implications for how to transform managers into leaders. Laurent suggests similar concepts tested within Orlando's *nurse-patient* relationship would align with the *leader-follower* relationship. We searched high and low but found there are no studies or research publications testing Laurent's proposed model, which was produced 20 years ago. Cardiff et al. (2018) proposed a conceptual framework specific to nursing, developed through participatory action research: *person-centered leadership*. As part of the development of this model, they created a graphic and a narrative representation of clinical nursing leadership as person-centered and relational. The strengths of a *person-centered leadership* framework are in alignment with other commonly used leadership styles such as servant leadership. However, person-centered leadership was developed with an "others-oriented" focus similar to servant leadership, which fails to recognize the leader's need to start with self. Also, the study conducted by Cardiff et al. was limited to one nursing unit within a hospital, thus creating a limited range of perspectives across settings and specialties. In conclusion, as we searched and read everything we could get our hands on in scholarly and mainstream literature, it became clear that these commonly used approaches all seemed to be missing a key player: the leader. Based on our decades of experience in frontline nursing leadership, we felt validated in discovering the literature aligned with our sense that nursing leaders who are effective but burn out quickly tend to not prioritize self-care. We made it our mission to learn more about leaders who are effective and are able to sustain healthy work environments for their teams.

Constructivist Grounded Theory

We'll try to make this section as painless as possible, but we need to share the basics of our approach and methods. Here goes! Constructivist grounded theory is a research paradigm that evolved from the epistemological underpinnings of Glaser and Strauss (1967), who revolutionized the methodology of grounded theory (Charmaz, 2008, 2014). Grounded theorists pursue frameworks that explain human issues entrenched in society. These are issues not formally named or identified rather they're human complexities sensed and brought to life through theoretical models that explain relationships between non-physical referents (Charmaz, 2014). Remember the wind? That's the basic premise of grounded theory. Put a name to something familiar yet uncharted. The beauty of constructivist grounded theory is the emphasis on the interrelationship between the researcher and participants in constructing shared meaning. The researcher's humanity is recognized as part of the research effort. Researchers are placed squarely within the methodology as an acknowledgement that their experience, expertise, and values are vital contributors to the research process and outcomes. This is the revolutionary aspect of constructivist versus traditional grounded theory. Traditional approaches advise researchers to be a tabula rasa, a blank slate, to attain theoretical sensitivity or stay above and outside the research process (Glaser, 1978). In contrast, the constructivist approach contends that theories should be influenced by the rich co-creative experience of participants, researchers, the literature, and the data. This means that as a constructivist grounded theory, Human-Centered Leadership draws on historical literature, the rich experiences of participants, data, and the abundant experience of the authors and researchers themselves, who have amassed nearly a century of experience in nursing.

The Nuts and Bolts

The population we focused on were nurses from the bedside to the boardroom who experienced nursing leadership either as the leader or as the person being led. Since this was a formal research project, we developed our proposal and received Internal Review Board (IRB) approval from an affiliated university. We then strategically activated our network of professional contacts across the region to gain a sample representative of nurse leaders at all levels: bedside, middle management, and executive leadership. The final sample included 39 nurse leaders in acute care organizations representing specialties including medical/surgical, obstetrics, perioperative, oncology, orthopedics, pediatrics, neonatology, nephrology, critical care, and administration. There were frontline nurses, charge nurses, clinical nurse specialists, unit level nurse managers, executive directors, and chief nursing officers. A snapshot of our nurse leaders revealed levels of experience ranging from 3 to 35 years, with an average of 20 years in the profession. The average age was 42.

We held face-to-face focus groups in neutral settings not associated with a particular organization or hospital. We obtained informed consent from each participant prior to starting the focus groups. The group interviews were facilitated by the authors, and we developed three levels of questions: starter questions (open-ended), intermediate questions (to expand on starter questions), and ending questions (to refine any remaining topics). Our aim was to provide open-ended questions that allowed natural dialogue to ensue. We used these questions to guide rich conversations and discussions around the social and psychological processes related to the participants' experiences in nursing, both as leaders and as those being led. Interestingly, we never got past the two opening questions in any focus group. The nurses were hungry to share their experiences and being in a group setting energized their passion for having their voices heard. The two starter questions were:

1. How would you describe a leader you would follow to the end of the earth?
2. How would you describe a nurse leader who, perhaps, has caused you to leave a position or move to another unit?

As you'll see in the narrative comments provided throughout this book, the participants were clearly able to identify positive and not-so-positive aspects of leaders throughout their careers.

The primary intention of the focus groups was to provide a safe space for sharing potentially traumatic as well as inspiring experiences. The group setting also provided an environment of shared experience in which ideas organically expanded into rich stories and narratives. Finally, the nurses were energetic about sharing their experiences, positive and negative. The prevailing feeling in the room was a sense of gratitude that someone was "finally" asking what a "good" nurse leader looks like. The participants also shared excitement at being part of something bigger than themselves, perhaps a revolution that might contribute to the scholarship of nursing, specifically nursing leadership. We were equally excited in the moment, with these nurses, as we realized we were "reigning in the wind." Nurses in the thick of practice and leadership were naming what we had all sensed was there. They named the leader who didn't seem to fit the mold of traditional, transformational, or servant leaders. They were describing and defining ways of being familiar to our collective nursing voice and experience. As researchers and nurses, ourselves, we heard our thoughts and ideas about leadership coming out of the mouths of others.

In the midst of such energizing group sessions, we prioritized recording the narratives through extensive field notes. We also made sure we confirmed that what we heard matched what the participants voiced by reading back to them, in the moment, their thoughts and ideas. We made sure we were accurately documenting their intentions. So, what did we do with all of those notes and data? First, we made sure we adhered to the constructivist coding process and conducted the research in a systematic and rigorous way. Coding is the process of assigning interpretive labels to ideas, constructs, or concepts that arise from the data (Carmichael & Cunningham, 2017; Saldaña, 2016). We used initial coding to map the nurses' "in vivo codes," which are unique phrases such as "walk the walk" or "a nurse's nurse." We then iteratively placed the nurses' responses (actual words and phrases) into a matrix that allowed categories to emerge, such as communication, support, and mindfulness. Please stay tuned and continue reading because, in the chapters that lie ahead, we'll be sharing specific words, stories, quotes, and the voices of these nurses to illustrate each of the concepts. Intermediate coding was the next step and resulted in 15 thematic attributes, which we then categorized to capture the essence of the nurses' ideas around positive and effective nursing leadership. Using advanced and final coding, the 15 attributes were then mapped into three dimensions identified within the theory: the Awakener, the Connector, and the Upholder. The culmination of this multi-year research journey resulted in the final logical connection between historical perspectives, the literature, the participants' voices, the data, and the researchers' placement within the process—the theory and model of Human-Centered Leadership in Healthcare (see Figure 1). The revolution officially began.

Figure 1

Human-Centered Leadership in Healthcare

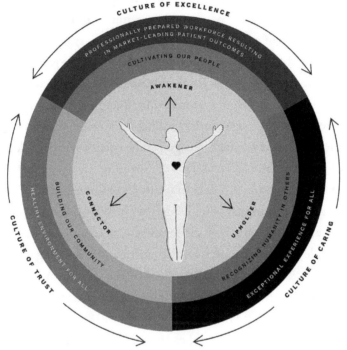

Note: From Leclerc L., Kennedy K., & Campis S. (2021). Human-centred leadership in health care: A contemporary nursing leadership theory generated via constructivist grounded theory. *Journal of Nursing Management*, 29, 294–306. https://doi.org/10.1111/jonm.13154.

The visual framework reflects an innovative approach to leadership in healthcare that starts with the leader's mind, body, and spirit as the locus of influence within local and larger complex systems. The Human-Centered Leader realizes success by connecting the leadership attributes of the Awakener, the Connector, and the Upholder to a Culture of Excellence, Trust, and Caring, which reflect industry-leading metrics.

Implications for Nurse Leaders

What is the connection between nursing leadership and patient outcomes? Does a relationship even exist? These are the million-dollar questions. Nurse leaders at all levels would be uniquely served by using a leadership style customized for and rooted in the essence of nursing. The nurses in the focus groups were energized to be part of a study that would shape a nursing-specific leadership theory. They described how using borrowed theories gets the job done but misses something in the end. One nurse, Jenna, described this mismatch as follows: "the humanity of our role to care for people when they're at their most vulnerable and the current trend to push harder and harder to meet numbers just doesn't jive." A human-centered approach recognizes the need to balance acknowledging nurses' and patients' humanity along with creating a culture that organically leads to the desired metrics. Leaders who cast a vision for nurses, their patients, their units, and their hospitals should start with themselves and pay attention to self-compassion, self-care, and self-awareness, because each leader not only sets the example, they set the pace for the health and well-being of their teams. From there, the leader can naturally influence change from the inside out by operationalizing the attributes of an Awakener, a Connector, and an Upholder (Leclerc et al., 2020; Porter-O'Grady & Malloch, 2018).

The theory of Human-Centered Leadership proposes that desired metrics for a Culture of Excellence, Trust, and Caring will organically follow the movement of a Human-Centered Leader (ANCC, 2015). In later chapters, we'll go into more detail about the connection between Human-Centered Leadership and metrics as we explore how the Awakener, the Connector, and the Upholder in each nurse leader can map their approach onto the metrics of excellence defined by the ANCC. Based on the results of our research and the constructivist grounded theory approach rooted in nurses' experiences, decades of experience that shaped the perspectives of the researchers, and the literature, there are potential connections (positive or causal) between the attributes and dimensions of Human-Centered Leadership approach and industry outcomes (Culture of Excellence, Trust, and Caring).

Nurse leaders should also consider taking part in a revolutionary movement to validate this nursing-specific leadership model by using the Human-Centered

Leadership theory as a framework for testing relationships between nursing leadership and outcomes. Nursing is over four million members strong and remains the largest part of the healthcare workforce in the United States and the world. Remember that hospital being built, the one we mentioned at the start of the book? Well, when it's complete and all the bells and whistles are in place, the most consistent humans in that place, 24/7/365, will be nurses. The steel beams in that shiny new or solid old hospital are the nurses, the ones at the bedside all the way to the ones in the executive suite. The invisible ties that hold up a healthcare team are the leaders. The profession and the world are primed for a nursing-specific leadership theory. The beauty of this theory and movement is that it's just the beginning. As we move forward, we're challenging nurse leaders to be part of building something bigger than ourselves. We'll be inviting each of you to test and use Human-Centered Leadership as a framework for frontline leadership at all levels and to validate successes with metrics of excellence. We'll be inviting you to be part of the revolution!

If you want to learn more about all the details of this research, please consider reading our detailed publication in the *Journal of Nursing Management*, an international, blind peer-reviewed publication for research on nursing leadership. Here's the reference:

Leclerc L., Kennedy K., & Campis, S. (2021). Human-centred leadership in health care: A contemporary nursing leadership theory generated via constructivist grounded theory. *Journal of Nursing Management*, 29, 294–306. https://doi.org/10.1111/jonm.13154

DISCUSSION QUESTIONS

1. Which leadership style have you historically identified with (servant, transformational, traditional)?
2. Have you taken part in a research project either as a researcher or a participant? Share your experience with the group.

REFLECTION

A revolution is a paradigm shift. It's when we change the way we think about something or approach something. When you consider a nursing leadership revolution for all nurses, from the bedside to the c-suite, what images and words come to mind?

_____

_____

_____

_____

_____

_____

REFERENCES

American Association of Colleges of Nursing. (2020). *DRAFT Essentials Domains, Descriptors, Contextual Statements, and Competencies.* https://www.aacnnursing.org/About-AACN/AACN-Governance/Committees-and-Task-Forces/Essentials

American Nurses Credentialing Center. (2015). *ANCC Magnet Recognition Program.* https://www.nursingworld.org/organizational-programs/magnet/

Bass, B. M. (1985). *Leadership and performance beyond expectations.* Free Press.

Burns, J. M. (1978). *Leadership* (1st ed.). Harper & Row.

Cardiff, S., McCormack, B., & McCance, T. (2018). Person-centred leadership: A relational approach to leadership derived through action research. *Journal of Clinical Nursing,* 27(15–16), 3056–3069. https://doi.org/10.1111/jocn.14492

Carmichael, T. & Cunningham, N. (2017). Theoretical data collection and data analysis with gerunds in a constructivist grounded theory study. *The Electronic Journal of Business Research Methods,* 15(2), 59–73.

Charmaz, K. (2008). *Grounded theory as an emergent method.* In S. Hesse-Biber, & P. Leavy (Eds.), *Handbook of emergent methods* (pp.155–172). Guildford Press.

Charmaz, K. (2014). *Constructing grounded theory* (2nd ed.). Sage.

Crowell, D. (2016). *Complexity leadership* (2nd ed.). F.A. Davis Company.

Glaser, B. G. (1978). Theoretical sensitivity: Advances in the methodology of grounded theory. Sociology Press.

Glaser, B. G., & Strauss, A. L. (1967). *The discovery of grounded theory*. Aldine.

Greenleaf, R. K. (1977). Servant leadership: A journey into the nature of legitimate power and *greatness*. Paulist Press.

Hall, H. H. (2015). An exploration of the relationship between servant leadership characteristics of nurse leaders and the perception of empowerment among their followers [Doctoral Dissertation, Indiana Wesleyan University]. ProQuest Networked Digital Library of Theses & Dissertations.

Han, K. Kim S. J. Jang, S. Kim, S. Lee, S. Y. Lee, H. J. & Park, E. (2015). Positive correlation between care given by specialists and registered nurses and improved outcomes for stroke patients. *Journal of the Neurological Sciences*, 353(1-2), 137–142. https://doi.org/10.1016/j.jns.2015.04.034

Lanaj, K., Johnson, R. E., & Lee, S. M. (2016). Benefits of transformational behaviors for leaders: A daily investigation of leader behaviors and need fulfillment. *Journal of Applied Psychology*, 101, 237–251.

Laurent, C. L. (2000). A nursing theory for nursing leadership. *Journal of Nursing Management*, 8, 83–87.

Leclerc L., Kennedy K., & Campis S. (2021). Human-centred leadership in health care: A contemporary nursing leadership theory generated via constructivist grounded theory. *Journal of Nursing Management*, 29, 294–306. https://doi.org/10.1111/jonm.13154

Lin, S., Scott, B. A., & Matta, F. K. (2019). The dark side of transformational leader behaviors for leaders themselves: A conservation of resources perspective. *Academy of Management Journal*, 62(5), 1556–1582. https://doi.org/10.5465/amj.2016.1255

Marquis, B. L., & Huston, C. J. (2017). *Leadership roles and management functions in nursing: Theory and application* (9th ed.). Wolters Kluwer Health.

O'Brien, M. E. (2011). Servant leadership in nursing: Spirituality and practice in contemporary health care. Jones and Bartlett.

Parris, D. L., & Peachey, J. W. (2013). A systematic literature review of servant leadership theory in organizational contexts. *Journal of Business Ethics*, 113, 377–393.

Porter-O'Grady, T. & Malloch, K. (2018). *Quantum leadership: Creating sustainable value in health care* (5th ed.). Jones & Bartlett.

Saldaña, J. (2016). *The coding manual for qualitative researchers*. Sage.

Weberg, D., & Fuller, R. (2019). Toxic leadership: Three lessons from complexity science to identify and stop toxic teams. *Nurse Leader*, 17(1), 22–26. https://doi.org/10.1016/j.mnl.2018.09.00

Weiss, S. A., Tappen, R. M., & Grimley, K. A. (2019). *Essentials of nursing leadership and management* (7th ed.). F. A. Davis Company.

RECOMMENDED READING

Donabedian A. (1966). Evaluating the quality of medical care. Milbank Memorial Fund Q. 1966; 44(3) (suppl),166-206. Reprinted in Milbank Q. 2005;83(4):691-729.

Donabedian A. (2002). *An introduction to quality assurance in health care*. Oxford University Press.

Singh, S. and Estefan, A. (2018). Selecting a grounded theory approach for nursing research. *Global Qualitative Nursing Research*, 5, 1–9.

Wong, C. A., Cummings, G. G., & Ducharme, L. (2013). The relationship between nursing leadership and patient outcomes: A systematic review update. *Journal of Nursing Management*, 21, 709–724.

PART II
IT STARTS WITH YOU

The Human-Centered Leader practices self-care, self-awareness, and mindfulness in order to build resiliency and the capacity to focus outward.

Chapter 3

The Human at the Center:
The Journey to Self-Awareness

"What is necessary to change a person is to change awareness of himself."
—Abraham Maslow, American Psychologist

M ost people have a fundamental understanding of what self-awareness is and the personal benefits associated with this attribute. Some people know that when we can see and understand ourselves honestly and clearly, we become more confident and creative people. When we are self-aware, we have the ability and desire to build stronger and more authentic relationships. As self-awareness grows, our communication with others becomes more intentional and effective. However, even though most people *believe* they are self-aware, organizational psychologist and researcher Tasha Eurich (2018) found that only 10–15% of the people she studied in her research actually fit the criteria.

When I was a new nurse manager, I had a rather painful "aha" moment one day when a colleague came to me and stated, in so many words, that she thought I had "changed" since becoming manager of the unit. I had worked as a bedside nurse on the unit for 15 years prior to accepting—reluctantly I might add—a formal leadership role. Her comment caught me completely off guard. "Changed?" I asked. "What do you mean?" She explained, "You used to be so happy and friendly and now you walk around so serious, and you don't talk to us anymore." Well, to say my feelings were hurt would be an understatement. I went home that day, partly mad, partly sad, and partly confused. The perception I had of myself in my new role was one of being serious, professional, and in control. I wanted to be perceived as a "strong, no-nonsense leader" who could get things done, but more importantly, I wanted to be a leader who would be taken seriously by other leaders. What the staff was seeing was someone completely different. They saw their new leader and colleague as someone who was suddenly aloof, unapproachable, and maybe taking herself a tad too seriously. The encounter with my colleague caused me to stop in my tracks and pause. I somehow found the courage I needed to examine the incident from the inside out. I realized there were some thoughts and behaviors I needed to acknowledge regarding how I thought effective leadership should look. This journey required me to dig deep within myself and address some of my insecurities, my fears, and my struggles with imposter syndrome. Throughout the process, I realized I had to accept my vulnerability, embrace my humanity, and learn to be truly present in the moment. I had to affirm, first within myself, that I brought something unique and beneficial to the table. This revelation, which came through a process of self-awareness and self-discovery, created a paradigm shift in the way I began to think about leadership and leadership success. By identifying, acknowledging, and accepting the behaviors and attitudes I needed to change within myself, I became more self-confident in my abilities and more authentic in my behaviors. I felt grateful to the colleague who pointed out her concerns. In many ways, her honesty helped me become a much more Human-Centered Leader by steering me towards developing a greater sense of my own self-awareness and authenticity.

To Know Thyself

So, let's ask the question—what does self-awareness have to do with Human-Centered Leadership in Healthcare? What does it mean "to know thyself"? According to Socrates, "to know thyself is the beginning of wisdom." It means having the ability to recognize different parts of your personality, including your thoughts and behaviors. The process involves being honest with yourself, acknowledging your strengths and your weaknesses, void of self-criticism. To know thyself means understanding what makes you happy and understanding what makes you stressed. Self-awareness is a learnable skill, however, it can be a hard and sometimes painful journey to develop that skill. The journey to self-awareness is an ongoing, lifelong process, and even though the importance of becoming a self-aware individual can't be minimized, many people, quite honestly, don't want to make the commitment. Most of us become satisfied and comfortable with our own personal status quos. We learn to deny or ignore some of our thoughts and behaviors because we don't want to openly and honestly address them. And then there are our two friends, blame and shame, that easily become the barriers that impede our ability to see ourselves as we are.

The Powerful Pursuit of Self-Awareness

According to Ghandi, "A man is but the product of his thoughts; what he thinks, he becomes." A paradigm is a way of thinking. It consists of a set of assumptions, concepts, behaviors, and beliefs that help define a view of reality. A paradigm shift occurs when there is a radical change in thought patterns and behaviors. Former ways of thinking and acting are replaced with new concepts. A paradigm shift can be compared to a personal revolution. As we all know, a revolution is a powerful and intentional act used to bring about change, whether politically or socially. A personal revolution is a powerful and intentional act used to bring about change within yourself. Personal change, when it is authentic and meaningful, comes when we create a paradigm shift—a revolution—in the way we think and act. Change occurs when the usual way of doing or thinking is replaced by new and different thoughts and actions, creating a shift in attitude, perception, behavior, and beliefs. The journey towards self-awareness requires us to do the individual and personal inner work that most of us tend to shy away from. No one likes to discover things about themselves that may be seen as weaknesses, but when we face our weaknesses and imperfections with humility and open-mindedness, we create a willingness within ourselves to learn, grow, and change. In his best-selling book *The 7 Habits of Highly Effective People,*

Steven Covey (2004) states that paradigms are powerful entities and embracing the power of the paradigm shift allows us to embrace quantum change both within ourselves and within our environments. He suggests focusing on understanding individual paradigms—our thoughts—begins with recognizing and understanding the innermost part of our being: our character, our values, and our motivations. Understanding individual paradigms involves embracing a proactive stance in acknowledging life events and owning our response to those events. Shedding light on our individual paradigms gives us the ability to embrace unique components of self-being and the aptness to understand one's thought processes, behaviors, and motivation factors.

A successful "inside out" approach starts when we first **acknowledge our vulnerabilities**. Brene Brown (2010), a well-known researcher and thought innovator, describes vulnerability as the courage to be present and seen in the moment, regardless of the outcome. It's not about having diminished capacity and should not be seen as a sign of weakness. Every human being is vulnerable. Vulnerability can't be avoided, even though it can be ignored. Brown says that acknowledging our vulnerabilities can lead to innovation, creativity and change. When we merge our vulnerabilities with our authentic selves, we might discover that our vulnerabilities become our greatest human connectors.

Second, we must **discover and develop our inner capabilities and strengths**. To accomplish this task in an authentic and thorough way, we must, third, **develop a strong sense of self**. So how do we do all this hard work? Keep reading!

The Four Self-Awareness Archetypes

Self-awareness is a crucial component to joy and success, both in our personal and professional lives. Eurich (2018) identified two categories of self-awareness. The first, she describes as *internal* self-awareness, which represents how well we know ourselves. She found that people who exhibited strong internal self-awareness felt happier, had higher job satisfaction, maintained stronger relationships, and exhibited more personal and social control. The second category she describes as *external* self-awareness, which represents how well we understand how we are perceived by others. Eurich's research showed that people with strong external self-awareness are skilled at showing empathy and are more open-minded to others' perspectives. Often, we assume if we're strong in one category of awareness, we will be strong in the second category. Eurich's research, however, found essentially no relationship between the two. From her research, she and her team identified four self-awareness archetypes that measure internal self-awareness against external self-awareness. *Introspectors* are those with a high internal self-awareness and a low external self-awareness. Eurich describes these people as having a strong and clear sense of who they are, but they are disinterested in searching for their blind spots or in getting feedback from others. The *Seekers*, according to Eurich, have a low external self-awareness and a low internal self-awareness. They don't have a sense of who they are, and they don't know how they are perceived by others. The *Pleasers* are those who have a high external self-awareness and a low internal self-awareness, which leads to their being so focused on how they are perceived by others that they may overlook what is important to them. The *Aware* are the fourth archetype, who are high in external self-awareness and high in internal self-awareness. These people know who they are yet value the opinions of others. Eurich concluded self-awareness consists of a delicate balance of these two distinct and often competing viewpoints. Our challenge is to find the courage to commit to the journey of increased self-awareness and true authenticity.

Self-awareness has been described by Bradberry and Greaves (2009), authors of *Emotional Intelligence 2.0*, as one of the core components of emotional intelligence and is seen as the foundation for personal growth. It involves understanding the underlying intentions steering our thoughts, actions, and behaviors and allows for the development of greater empathy for others, improved listening and critical thinking skills, development of strong relationships, and enhanced leadership capabilities. Self-awareness allows us to live in the place of integrity and authenticity, becoming connected to experiences and relationships in order to understand how we are received and perceived.

Figure 2

The Four Self-Awareness Archetypes

	Low external self-awareness	High external self-awareness
High internal self-awareness	**INTROSPECTORS** They're clear on who they are but don't challenge their own views or search for blind spots by getting feedback from others. This can harm their relationships and limit their success.	**AWARE** They know who they are, what they want to accomplish, and seek out and value others' opinions. This is where leaders begin to fully realize the true benefits of self-awareness
Low internal self-awareness	**SEEKERS** They don't yet know who they are, what they stand for, or how their teams see them. As a result, they might feel stuck or frustrated with their performance and relationships.	**PLEASERS** They can be so focused on appearing a certain way to others that they could be overlooking what matters to them. Over time, they tend to make choices that aren't in service of their own success and fulfillment.

Note. This 2x2 grid maps internal self-awareness (how well you know yourself) against external self-awareness (how well you understand how others see you). Reprinted from Eurich, T. (2018, January 4). *What self awareness really is (and how to cultivate it) Managing Yourself.* https://hbr.org/2018/01/what-self-awareness-is-and-how-to-cultivate-it

American psychologists Joseph Luft and Harrington Ingham, (1955) developed a technique for improving self-awareness known as the Johari Window Model. The Johari Window model, referred to by Chapman (2003) as a model for self-awareness based on feedback and disclosure, is a simple tool that can be used by individuals and teams to develop self-awareness and personal growth, along with interpersonal relationships and team building. The model is a diagram consisting of four "panes" representing information about the self that is both known and unknown to the individual, along with information about the individual that is known and unknown to others. The model is based on two assumptions: by revealing information to others, you acquire their trust, and through feedback from others, you learn about yourself.

Table 1

The Johari Window Model

	Known to Self	Unknown to Self
Known to Others	**OPEN SELF** Information about you that both you and others know.	**BLIND SELF** Information about you that you don't know but others do know.
Unknown to Others	**HIDDEN SELF** Information about you that you know but others don't know.	**UNKNOWN SELF** Information about you that neither you nor others know.

Note: Adapted from Chapman, A. (2003). Johari Window: A model for self-awareness, personal development, group development and understanding relationships. Retrieved from: https://apps.cfli.wisc.edu/johari/support/JohariExplainChapman2003.pdf

Quadrant 1 is referred to as the **Open Self** and reflects information about you, such as attitudes, emotions, experiences, and knowledge, which is known by you and by the team. This area is a space where teams are most productive and effective. Communication is effective and the team is free from distractions and conflict. This space is where there is plenty of cooperation between people and trust is high.

Quadrant 2 is the **Blind Spot** area and reflects what is known about you by others but is unknown to you. This is a space that is neither productive nor effective for you or for others. This is the area where honest and authentic feedback from others can help you grow and develop self-awareness. Let's go back to my "aha" moment. During this time of my life, I was obviously lacking some self-awareness skills. With my skewed understanding of what leadership should look like, I unconsciously changed my behaviors. I went from being seen as friendly to being perceived as aloof and from collaborative to unapproachable. I, quite honestly, was not aware of these changes in my behavior and in the way people were perceiving me. I had developed blind spots. A blind spot is pretty much what the name implies. It is an area that you can't see easily, and your behavior becomes limited by what you don't know.

Blind spots have been described as the "unknown unknowns," and regardless of how well we think we know ourselves, most times we are clueless about some of our traits and behaviors. Curiously enough, however, blind spots are always visible to others. Gustavo Razzeffi (2018), change instigator and author, identifies four main types of blind spots. **Knowledge blindness** is the inability to evaluate one's competence in an objective manner. This bias causes people of low ability to suffer from "illusory superiority," and this can cause a person to feel overconfident until someone or something proves them wrong. **Beliefs blindness**, also referred to as "confirmation bias," encourages us to take sides by embracing information and ideas that support our beliefs and rejecting ideas and information that contradict them. This type of blindness prevents one from seeing ideas and information from a different perspective. The third type of blindness Razzeffi identifies is **emotional blindness**. Emotions steer our focus to one aspect of reality and can hinder perceptions. Emotions are effective in expressing a part of oneself, but emotions don't have to define who you are as a person. **Thoughts blindness** is the belief that you are always right, on one end of the spectrum, or being overly judgmental about yourself, on the other. Both thought processes can lead to a life of inauthenticity. Blind spots can be vulnerable areas for leaders. Behaviors, such as not asking for help, avoiding difficult conversations, having an "I know best" attitude, blaming others, and accepting low performance standards are all examples of blind spots that are seen frequently in leaders. Developing self-awareness can help us begin to see that every blind spot has a flip side, and this flip side can become a strength and an opportunity for growth.

Quadrant 3 is referred to as the **Hidden Self** and reflects things we know about ourselves but keep hidden from others. There are many reasons we choose to keep things hidden from others, but keep in mind, self-awareness is not about becoming an open book for all to see. When we can learn to self-disclose or share *relevant* information with others, the **Open Self** (Quadrant 1) can grow and strengthen. What to share and when to share it is a personal decision.

Finally, **Quadrant 4,** the **Unknown Self** is the quadrant where information, feelings, and aptitudes—hidden talents—are unknown both to you and to others. This can be considered the quadrant of true personal growth and self-discovery and can lead to a stronger sense of self-awareness. Feedback and constructive observation from others are two effective tools to help in this area.

The journey to self-awareness is not an easy one. It requires courage and initiative. Initiative challenges us to act, to stay grounded and focused, and to practice self-discipline. We need courage because self-discovery can be scary, especially when we uncover thoughts and behaviors that need to change. Self-awareness is often seen as a personal journey, however, feedback from others, even when it may be uncomfortable, can help unlock one's self-knowledge, especially when there is a desire to grow. Soliciting feedback and surrounding yourself with diverse thinkers who you are willing to learn from can help flip those annoying blind spots or can help identify hidden talents. Developing and nurturing a strong sense of self-awareness requires practicing mindfulness and being able to acknowledge your inner calm.

Mindfulness incites us to be present in the moment and encourages us to avoid worrying about yesterday and dreading tomorrow. Your inner calm is the place deep inside that allows for a pause. During this pause, the inner calm that is within each of us arises to help us regroup, rethink, and recharge. Being mindful and possessing inner calm allows us to confront change and disruption without fear. As self-awareness grows, the ability to face and accept the present reality becomes a key to authentic well-being. The paradigm shift—the personal revolution—begins with an "inside out" perspective; we must create and nurture the authentic and emotional connection to ourselves first—*it starts with you*—and second, to others—*but it's not about you.* "Inside out" implies starting first with self, with the innermost part of you—your thoughts, your actions, your values, and your motives. The "authentic self" has been described as living a life that is in line with one's core values, and reflects the real, true, and genuine aspects of who we are. In her best-selling book *The Gifts of Imperfection*, Brené Brown (2010) describes authenticity as a daily practice of letting go of who we think we are supposed to be and embracing who we are. This mindset involves a collection of conscious choices regarding how we want to live our lives. Authenticity is about being true to yourself. Our authentic self allows us to live our lives according to our values and our purpose. Brown explains that choosing authenticity requires the courage to be imperfect in a world that sometimes expects perfection, developing a compassion for self, and nurturing your connection to others. These are daily choices.

Humans are complex beings. We have different thoughts, reactions, and motivators, and these differences make us unique. What we have in common is our connection to each other. Leadership is about inspiring, guiding, and encouraging people to be their best selves, but more importantly, leadership is about the way we choose to lead our lives. The Human-Centered Leadership paradigm understands that leadership is not just something one does. Leadership reflects and exemplifies who we are at our core. The Human-Centered Leadership model suggests that to understand, lead, and care for others, we must understand, lead, and care for ourselves first. The Human-Centered Leadership approach also asserts that when the leader focuses on self first, the attributes of the Awakener, the Connector, and the Upholder begin to emerge, and a culture of caring, trust, and excellence is created. Putting our humanity at the center of leadership and using our self-awareness as the cornerstone, enables us to improve our capacity for physical, emotional, mental, and spiritual well-being. Leaders must look inward and embrace self-care, self-compassion, and mindfulness to increase their resiliency and their capacity to focus outward.

I have always loved an inspirational challenge, often attributed to Mahatma Gandhi, to be the change you want to see in the world, however, this is a common way to paraphrase a more profound and meaningful version of his original quote. Gandhi's (1913, as quoted in Ranseth, 2015) actual quote is

> We but mirror the world. All the tendencies present in the outer world are to be found in the world of our body. If we could change ourselves, the tendencies in the world would also change. As a man changes his own nature, so does the attitude of the world change towards him. This is the divine mystery supreme. A wonderful thing it is and the source of our happiness. We need not wait to see what others do.

Gandhi's words reveal a powerful truth suggesting life changes are inevitable and can be found all around us. What we see in the world, in our environments, and in our relationships is no more and no less a reflection of what is inside of ourselves. His words challenge us to commit to individual reflection and growth in order to live life as a more enlightened, resilient, and self-aware person. In other words, be the person who looks for growth and change in self first, and growth and change in others will follow.

In conclusion, my "aha" moment can be defined as the moment I paused and took time to reflect on my thoughts, beliefs, and behaviors as a leader. I acknowledged my blind spots, accepted my feelings of vulnerability, and then took the courageous initiative to make changes in my thoughts and behaviors related to what I had perceived as "successful leadership." I realized successful leadership is not being at the top and looking down; it is about being immersed in the middle and looking outward. The change in my thoughts and behaviors as a result of establishing a stronger sense of self-awareness encouraged new feelings of trust and confidence from the staff and provided me with the ability to move forward in obtaining the outcomes that reflected excellent patient care.

Successful leadership is not being at the top and looking down; it is about being immersed in the middle and looking outward.

To know yourself is a journey that is unpredictable. It's a journey that can put us face-to-face with our deepest fears, our vulnerabilities, and our self-doubts. It's a journey that teaches us to respect our weaknesses and our strengths, our likes and our dislikes, our passions and our fears. In the words of Erik Erikson (1998), "The more you know yourself, the more patience you have for what you see in others. (para. 16)" It starts with you…

DISCUSSION QUESTIONS

1. How can we make cultivating self-awareness an everyday practice?
2. What are your real and perceived barriers in becoming self-aware?
3. What is your definition of vulnerability, and do you believe that vulnerable leaders make good leaders? Why?

4. According to Dr. Eurich's definitions of self-awareness, which archetype do you most identify with and why?

REFLECTION

What would my journey towards self-awareness look like? How would becoming more self-aware benefit me as a leader?

_____

_____

_____

_____

_____

_____

REFERENCES

Bradberry, T., Greaves, J. (2009). *Emotional intelligence 2.0.* TalentSmart.

Brown, B. (2010). *The gifts of imperfection: Let go of who you think you're supposed to be and embrace who you are.* Hazelden Publishing.

Chapman, A. (2003). *Johari Window: A model for self-awareness, personal development, group development and understanding relationships.* Retrieved from: https://apps.cfli.wisc.edu/johari/support/JohariExplainChapman2003.pdf

Covey, S. R. (2004). *7 habits of highly effective people.* Simon and Schuster.

Erikson, E. (1998, June 14). Erikson, in His Own Old Age, Expand His View of Life [Interview]. The New York Times—Daniel Goleman. https://archive.nytimes.com/www.nytimes.com/books/99/08/22/specials/erikson-old.html#:~:text="The%20more%20you%20know%20yourself,%20the%20more%20patience,becomes,%20too,%20a%20sense%20of%20humor%20about%20life.

Eurich, T. (2018, January 4). *What Self Awareness Really Is (and how to cultivate it) Managing Yourself.* https://hbr.org/2018/01/what-self-awareness-is-and-how-to-cultivate-it

Luft, J. and Ingham, J. (1955). *The Johari window, a graphic model of interpersonal awareness.* Proceedings of the Western Training Laboratory in Group Development. Los Angeles: University of California, Los Angeles.

Ranseth, J. (2015, August 27). "Gandhi didn't actually ever say 'Be the change you want to see in the world.' Here's the real quote…" https://josephranseth.com/gandhi-didnt-say-be-the-change-you-want-to-see-in-the-world/

Razzeffi, G. (2019, March 25). *How to conquer your blind spots.* https://www.fearlessculture.design-/blog-posts/how-to-conquer-your-blind-spots

RECOMMENDED READING

Brown, B. (2018). *Dare to lead: brave work, tough conversations, whole hearts.* Penguin Random House.

Eurich, T. (2020). *The Insight Quiz. How self-aware are you? Take the quiz to find out!* https://www.insight-book.com/quiz

Chapter 4

The Importance of Self-Care and Self-Compassion in a World Full of Burnout

"You can't pour from an empty cup. Take care of yourself first."
—Author Unknown

When I was a novice nurse, one of the more senior nurses spoke to me openly and candidly about nursing stress and nursing burnout. She told me story after story of nurses who went through periods of physical, mental, and emotional exhaustion, many choosing to leave the bedside after only a few years. I knew and accepted that nursing was a stressful and challenging profession, but I was surprised to hear so many stories where nurses seemed to be suffering from extreme stress and burnout. I remember thinking to myself that burnout would never happen to me. I considered myself to be a person who managed stress well. However, what I learned after years as a bedside nurse was that stress can happen instantaneously, but burnout creeps up over time, sometimes quietly zapping energy and diluting passion. Many years into my career, I hit a wall. I found myself dreading going to work. I was chronically tired. I lost my passion for what I was doing, both at home as a wife and mother and at the hospital. I became disengaged and frustrated. I began experiencing insomnia, loss of appetite, and headaches. I knew I was not physically sick, but my sense of well-being was taking a beating. In other words, my cup was empty.

So, let's talk about stress. Stress enters our life when the expectations and demands of life, work, or relationships and our coping abilities are out of balance. Stressors can come from internal or external forces and, if not addressed, can lead to anxiety and fear. Internal forces, such as self-imposed expectations that are unrealistic, unhealthy, and uncompromising—some call this perfectionism— can lead to stress. This type of stress is self-inflicted and can lead to the internal struggles of negative self-talk, depleted self-esteem, and feelings of being unworthy. External forces such as toxic work environments or dysfunctional relationships can also lead to stress. Sometimes there are events that are stressful in nature and are out of our control. These "impersonal" stressors can include things like pandemics or an unstable economy. Regardless of where it originates, stress, when left unchecked, can negatively affect the mind, the body, and the spirit. Stress automatically activates the flight-or-fight systems in the body, which is the body's way of protecting us in the face of threats, whether real or perceived. With stress, there is an overreaction of emotions and an increased sense of urgency, which is often accompanied by a lack of energy and fatigue. Unfortunately, the stress-activated response, which involves both the brain and the body, does not differentiate between physical and emotional threats or threats that are real versus imagined. There are two categories of stress, acute and chronic. Acute stress is stress that is short term and is typically a part of everyday life. Our body adapts well to acute stress, and some experts even state that acute stress is not considered harmful because it keeps our normal stress response primed and ready. Experiencing the constant state of heightened awareness that comes with chronic stress is a lot like a bad habit. Chronic stress can revamp the brain, leaving one open to feelings of increased anxiety, fear, and additional stress. Scientists feel that chronic stress and the activation and overuse of stress hormones can negatively affect the body, leading to cardiovascular disease, high blood pressure, and even type 2 diabetes. When we experience chronic exposure to stress, our attitudes, relationships, work productivity, and overall health are negatively affected.

So, What's the Difference Between Stress and Burnout?

Many people experience episodes of stress and fatigue, and even though it can be a difficult moment to get through, it's often viewed as temporary. If, however, stress becomes chronic, an increased risk of burnout exists. Burnout has been described as the body's response to the behavior of putting out a lot of effort, both physical and mental, without taking in what you need to balance and restore yourself. Think of the empty cup analogy. Symptoms of burnout can include feeling overwhelmed or disillusioned with things that used to bring joy and excitement. Physical symptoms of burnout can involve having a heavy feeling of constant dread in your stomach, chronic fatigue, and memory loss. A sense of hopelessness or despair can begin to creep in when that cup called life is being drained and there is nothing in place to refill it.

Burnout is a commonly used term within the world of nursing, and the phenomenon of burnout has been researched and studied by many over the last few years. The term "burnout" was coined by American psychologist Herbert Freudenberger, in the mid-1970s and is used to describe the mental and physical exhaustion experienced by people who are overly stressed within their work environments. The physical and emotional fatigue that accompanies burnout can lead to a decrease in or loss of motivation for work that evolves into a sense of personal and professional failure (Oliveira, 2019). "Nurse burnout" is becoming an all-too-common concern in healthcare. In a 2017 survey by Kronos Incorporated, 98% of hospital nurses stated that their work is physically and mentally demanding, 85% of the nurses noted that their nursing jobs led to overall feelings of fatigue, and 63% of nurses reported feeling burnout at some point during their careers. While most nurses experience stress at work due to heavy workloads, long hours, increased physical demands, moral distress, workplace violence, and feelings of disempowerment, burnout reflects the intense physical and emotional side effects caused by that stress. Burnout conjures images of disengagement, physical and mental exhaustion, a diminished sense of achievement, both personally and professionally, and perhaps even apathy. Stress and burnout can directly affect one's well-being by depleting the necessary resources required for resiliency and coping. The American Nurses Association (ANA) recognizes the importance of self-care in the face of stress and addresses the responsibility of the professional nurse in the ANA Code of Ethics (2015). The Code of Ethics, Provision 5, states "the nurse owes the same duty to self as to others, including the responsibility to promote health and safety, preserve wholeness of character and integrity, maintain competence and continue personal and professional growth." Provision 5.2 breaks down this responsibility even further, stating:

Nurses should model the same health maintenance and health promotion measures that they teach and research, obtain healthcare when needed, and avoid taking unnecessary risks to health or safety in the course of their professional and personal activities. Fatigue and compassion fatigue affect a nurse's performance and personal life. To mitigate these effects, eat a healthy diet, exercise, get sufficient rest, maintain personal relationships, engage in adequate leisure and activities, and attend to spiritual or religious needs. The satisfying work must be held in balance to promote and own health and well-being.

Self-care and well-being mean different things to different people, but at the end of the day, self-care and well-being are all about keeping your cup filled.

Self-Care and the Art of Resiliency

Self-care, what exactly is it and how will it benefit me? Self-care is not a new concept and has certainly, over recent years, become a popular topic for discussion. Some people, however, misunderstand the concept of self-care and often confuse it with self-improvement. Self-improvement is based on a mindset that says, "something is wrong with me and I need to fix it" or "I lack something, and I need figure out how to develop it." Even though self-improvement may start out with positive goals, when those goals are not achieved, or if perfection is not reached, shame, blame, and negative self-talk can sometimes take over (Brown, 2010). Self-care, on the other hand, is all about being present in the moment, nurturing the body, mind, and spirit in the here and now. Self-care reflects the way **we treat ourselves** and includes any activity that we deliberately do to take care of our physical, mental, and emotional health. Self-care is not a selfish or self-indulgent act, and it is not about adding any more items to an already overloaded to-do list. It is about establishing intentional and individualized daily habits—yes, I said habits—that nurture and support our overall sense of well-being. Research has shown that adding a healthy dose of self-care into our daily routine reduces stress, increases productivity, and allows us to approach life with a happy body and mind.

Self-Care in Action

1. Eat mindfully: take away the distractions and enjoy your meal.
2. Move your body: run, walk, skip, or dance, just move.
3. Unplug from social media occasionally: avoid the "rabbit hole."
4. Create a cozy and safe space that will encourage rest and relaxation.
5. Laugh: it really is the best medicine.
6. Give yourself permission to be creative—then create!
7. Express gratitude: honor the small and the big influencers in your life.

Most people understand that a daily practice of self-care involves adhering to a healthy diet, following an exercise regimen, getting enough quality sleep, and maintaining work/life balance. However, many people have a skewed view of self-care and, in many cases, consider self-care as a form of self-indulgence. Just for the record, an indulgence is defined as a luxury. When self-care is considered an indulgence, for whatever reason, we are claiming that caring for ourselves is a luxury versus a necessity. It means that we allow ourselves to indulge in the practices of self-care on occasion. This kind of thinking is just wrong! Self-care is not an indulgence. Self-care is a discipline. It is a habit. Self-care is something you do every single day, not just when your world gets crazy or when you find yourself with some extra time on your hands. Practicing self-care is a choice. It is making a commitment to nurture habits that allow you to stay healthy and balanced. When you take care of yourself first, when you make disciplined choices, you are in a much better position to take care of others. You have the energy, both physically and mentally, to approach your work and your life with meaning and purpose. Self-care, at its core, is about making sure you are caring for your body and your mind, making you a more solid and healthy person who doesn't sweat the small stuff.

We all know that when life gets busy and chaotic, our sense of well-being is affected. During times like these, self-care is a vital tool in helping strengthen our resiliency. You may ask, what does the practice of self-care have to do with resiliency? When I was a little girl, one of my favorite toys was a big balloon that had a rubber handle tied to it. The object of this toy was to hold on to the rubber handle, which was essentially a rubber band, and punch the balloon away from you. No matter how hard or fast I punched the balloon, it always bounced back. I think of this toy and how it relates to resiliency. Rubber bands have often been used as a metaphor to describe resiliency. Rubber bands are strong, flexible, durable, and hard to break. Resiliency has been described as the ability to recover quickly from a difficult or challenging situation. The rubber band handle on this toy allows for the balloon to "bounce back." However, if the balloon is low on air, it doesn't bounce back as quickly, no matter how strong the rubber band. The balloon represents self-care, and if we aren't committed to practicing self-care on a daily basis, we, too, lose air and can't back bounce as quickly. Resiliency, at its core, demands that we be emotionally flexible, adaptable, and positive in our outlook. We can't be any of these things if we don't practice habits of daily self-care.

If you pay attention, you will see that resilient people not only practice self-care, but they also understand and embrace the benefits. Resilient people understand that resiliency comes from within, and nurture themselves with healthy food habits, positive thoughts, feelings of gratitude, and usually surround themselves with positive people. Resilient people are usually more energetic and motivated because they commit to self-care practices on a daily basis. They also tend to have a higher sense of self-awareness and self-compassion and may be thought of as more emotionally intelligent. Being a resilient person doesn't mean you won't experience life's challenges or that you won't feel life's disappointments. Everyone experiences life's twists and turns, but how well we adapt in the face of difficulties is what defines resiliency. Resilient people tend to see themselves in the survivor role rather that the victim role and tend to have an ability to affect the outcome of an experience through personal action. Psychologists call this their "internal locus of control," which involves learning and developing certain thoughts and behaviors that allow you to "bounce back" after experiencing a difficult or challenging circumstance. It requires time and it requires focus, but the good news is that resiliency is a trait anyone can learn. The American Psychological Association (2012) suggests several attributes are necessary in order to develop and nurture a resilient spirit. One attribute is the **ability to maintain healthy and positive relationships**. Connecting with people who are trustworthy, empathetic, and who validate our feelings reminds us that we are not alone.

I have a sister who lives in another city. We have both struggled with the feelings of loneliness and isolation the COVID-19 pandemic has brought to all of us. One morning in early July, my sister called me feeling sad and anxious. She just wanted to talk to someone she trusted. I happened to be taking a walk when she called, so I told her to put on her shoes and join me. We spent over an hour talking to each other. We talked about everything, nothing was off the table, and four miles later, we felt connected and validated. Both of us felt better emotionally and physically when we hung up. We have since made our "Walk and Talk" a daily habit. The connection we have made has strengthened our relationship and the resiliency needed to get through this challenging and isolating time.

The second attribute in helping increase resiliency involves **acknowledging and accepting the notion that there are some circumstances that are out of our control**. We don't need to use our energy to focus on fixing things we have no control over. Steven M. Southwick and Dennis Charney (2012), authors of the book *Resilience: The Science of Mastering Life's Greatest Challenges*, write that resiliency occurs when people can assess a difficult situation and find the meaningful opportunities within it. The ability to accept reality, focus energy on positive potential, keep a sense of perspective, and accept change as a part of life, strengthens our ability to become resilient individuals.

Self-Care Versus Self-Compassion: The Chicken or the Egg?

Did you know that the human brain creates around 60,000–80,000 thoughts per day? That is, on average, about 48 thoughts per minute. Do your thoughts tell you how beautiful or smart you are, or how your decisions were "spot on"? If you are like most, the answer to that question is a resounding NO! We are all aware of that little voice inside our head, the one that seems to second-guess our decisions or hurls negative comments and insults our way. Why does that little voice have so much power and influence over the way we feel about ourselves? I can't tell you how many times that little voice has woken me from a deep sleep, just to remind me how inadequate I am. I jokingly call it "the monkey on my shoulder." For many years, I never disputed what this monkey was telling me. In fact, I believed almost everything it said. Over time, I began to see how this little monkey's negative talk was affecting every aspect of my life, and I began to see how this little negative voice influenced the way I felt about myself. Most of us grew up hearing about the Golden Rule: *Treat people like you want to be treated.* It's a concept that's simple and to the point, right? But what if we flipped it to say, *Treat yourself as kindly as you treat others*? Why does this become more of a challenge? After all, that little voice inside your head is you talking to you! We say things to ourselves that we would never say to a friend or to someone we cared about. Why? Could it be that we go down the rabbit hole of perfectionism? Do we feel like we need to be perfect in all things in order to be perceived as relevant or worthy? How does self-compassion become an integral part of self-care?

Leading expert and researcher on self-compassion, Dr. Kristen Neff (2021) says that having compassion for self is really no different than having compassion for others. Neff says that when we show compassion to others, we first, notice their suffering; second, we respond to the pain with empathy and non-judgement; and finally, we understand and accept that suffering, pain and imperfection are part of the human experience. Showing compassion to ourselves involves these same three things. Neff (2021, para. 2) explains,

> Instead of mercilessly judging and criticizing yourself for various inadequacies or shortcomings, self-compassion means you are kind and

understanding when confronted with personal failings-after all, who ever said you were supposed to be perfect? Perhaps most importantly, having compassion for yourself means that you honor and accept your humanness.

There is no such thing as being perfect. It doesn't exist. Perfection is an unattainable goal. Perfectionism is a way of thinking, not a way of being. Overcoming the desire for perfectionism can be a challenge. It requires us to stop, breath, and realize that we are vulnerable, imperfect human beings living in a world with other vulnerable imperfect human beings. When we can see and acknowledge our human-ness we can begin the journey towards self-compassion.

Author Jack Kornfield (1994) argues, "If your compassion does not include yourself, it is incomplete" (p. 28). Self-compassion reflects the way **we relate to ourselves**, and while self-care is about *doing*, self-compassion is about *thinking* and *feeling*. You show yourself compassion when you can view and acknowledge your life struggles with understanding, kindness, and grace. You give yourself the benefit of the doubt instead of using negative self-talk to undermine your intentions. You show yourself compassion when you realize that you did your best, even if it isn't perfect. As psychologist Hara Estroff Marano (2010) explains, "Perfectionism may be the ultimate self-defeating behavior. It turns people into slaves of success but keeps them focused on failure, dooming them to a lifetime of doubt and depression. (para.1)" Perfectionism ties self-worth to achieving unattainable standards. In *The Gifts of Imperfection*, Brown (2010) states that where perfectionism exists, shame is always lurking. She describes perfectionism as self-destructive and addictive; eventually it leads to feeling shamed, judged, and blamed for not being "good enough." She says the ability to acknowledge our vulnerabilities will help us develop a resistance to the shame-game. Self-compassion is not self-pity and does not reflect self-indulgence. Self-compassion is the ability to embrace ourselves, just like we would embrace our friend, with kindness and understanding and without judgement.

Do you remember the question: which came first, the chicken or the egg? I know when I was growing up, trying to answer that question was one of the all-time favorite debates to have with my friends. It is a fun question to debate, but it also points to an inherent truth—the chicken or the egg metaphor simply describes situations where it isn't clear which of two events should be considered the cause and which should be considered the effect. Consider this, do we develop self-compassion because we practice self-care, or do we practice self-care because we show ourselves self-compassion? In the end, does it really matter? Self-compassion and self-care, whether chicken or egg, are both vitally important to our well-being. Both are associated with greater emotional resilience and self-awareness, and isn't that what really matters?

DISCUSSION QUESTIONS

1. Do you perceive self-care as an indulgence or a necessity? Why? How do you define self-care?
2. What are some examples of self-care that you use?
3. Have you experienced burnout in your career? If so, what did it look like for you?

REFLECTION

Think about a time when you were extra hard on yourself, for example a time when you made a poor choice or made a mistake. Now imagine your best friend experienced the same thing. How would you talk differently to your friend than you did to yourself?

_____

_____

_____

_____

_____

_____

REFERENCES

American Psychological Association. (2012). *Building your resilience.* American Psychological Association. https://www.apa.org/topics/resilience

Brown, Brené. (2010). *The Gifts of Imperfection.* Hazelden Publishing.

Marano, H. E. (2010). Pitfalls of Perfectionism. Psychology Today, Online. http://www.psychologytoday.com/articles/200802/pitfalls-perfectionism

Kornfield, J. (1994). *Buddha's Little Instruction Book.* Bantam.

Kronos Incorporated. (2017) Employee Engagement in Nursing. Retrieved from https://www.businesswire.com/news/home/20170508005305/en/Kronos-Survey-Finds-Nurses-Love-Fatigue-Pervasive

Marano, H.E. (2020, 15 April). *Pitfalls of perfectionism.* Psychology Today Web.

Neff, K. (2021). *Definition and Three Elements of Self Compassion.* https://www.emotionalaffair.org/wp-content/uploads/2012/10/Self-compassion.pdf

Oliveira, S.M, Sousa, L.V., Gadelha, M., & Nascimento, V. (2019, March 29). Prevention of actions of burnout syndrome in nurses: An integrating literature review. *Clinical Pract Epidem Ment Health,* 15 64-73.

Southwick, S. & Charney, D. (2012). *Resilience: the science of mastering life's greatest challenges.* Cambridge University Press.

RECOMMENDED READING

Neff, K. (2015). *Self-compassion: The proven power of being kind to yourself.* HarperCollins Publishers.

Scala, E. & Drummond, D. (2016). *Stop nurse burnout: what to do when working harder isn't working.* Heritage Press Publications.

Skinner, J. (2015). *Nursing by heart: transformational self-care for nurses.* Ayni Books, John Hunt Publishing.

Chapter 5

Two Tigers, a Mouse, and a Strawberry: The Art of Mindfulness

"Mindfulness means paying attention in a particular way, on purpose, in the present moment, non-judgmentally."
—**Jon Kabat-Zin** (2017), American Professor of Medicine
emeritus at the University of Massachusetts Medical School
and Founder of Mindfulness-Based Stress Reduction

A parable shared by Gregory Angell in 2017, entitled "A Story About Living in the Present Moment" tells of a man, who, after being chased by a tiger, falls from a cliff. He grabs hold of a vine in order to save himself from falling further. When he looks up, he notices the tiger that had been chasing him is there, at the top of the cliff, snarling and baring his teeth. When he looks down, he sees another tiger, pacing back and forth, looking up at him. While he is holding on for dear life, a mouse comes out of the crevices of the cliff and begins to gnaw on the vine. The man tries to shoo it away, but it keeps gnawing. For a moment, the man is paralyzed with fear. He looks up, he looks down, and he looks up again. In his moment of pure panic, he stops, he takes a deep breath and looks to his right. There, not an arm's length away, he sees a bright, red, plump strawberry. He reaches over and plucks the berry. He holds it in his hands, takes a bite and finds it delicious. He closes his eyes and enjoys the moment. He feels the warmth of the sun on his face, the slight breeze in his hair, and the sweetness of the strawberry on his lips. The story Angell tells is one of metaphors and symbolism. For instance, the tiger at the top of the cliff represents the past. The past may appear scary and threatening, but there is no way to "climb back up the cliff" to address that tiger, and though he may appear scary, he is no longer a threat. The tiger at the foot of the cliff represents the future, and even though it is a tiger, there are a lot of unknowns on how that tiger might react. It paces back and forth, but it doesn't appear angry or on the verge of attack, and it is not necessarily beneficial to waste time worrying about how it will react. In Angell's story, the mouse represents time, and time always "gnaws" at us, right? What I appreciate about this story is the behavior of the man. As anxious and stressed as he is, he allows himself to pause, breathe, and refocus on his situation. He mindfully places himself in the moment. He notices the beauty of the cliff and acknowledges his luck in grabbing the vine. In the midst of his strife, he finds a beautiful, tasty strawberry to enjoy. The man acknowledges the past, recognizes the future, and understands the importance of time, but more importantly, he becomes aware of the moment. Have you ever felt yourself on that "cliff" of life, worrying about yesterday and dreading tomorrow, feeling like there is not enough time?

The art of mindfulness is the process of purposely bringing attention and awareness to experiences occurring in the present moment. It is the ability to be fully present, aware of where we are, aware of what we are doing, and not feeling overly judgmental or overwhelmed by what is happening around us. Attempting to stay peaceful and calm during times of incredible stress, fear, or agitation can seem impossible, and this is understandable. As nurses, we have chosen to work in an environment that is often seen as chaotic, demanding, and stressful. We are constantly on the lookout for all of the things that could go wrong, and this hypervigilance, which can sometimes lead to harmful self-criticism, keeps us from achieving our full potential as nurses and nurse leaders. Mindfulness is an important aspect of self-care, self-compassion, and is directly related to self-awareness. It allows us to address and get rid of the disquiet that can sometimes invade our minds.

Mindfulness is an active process that, when practiced, trains and strengthens parts of the brain that receive little to no training. Most of us are aware of the benefits of physical exercise. We know that when we train our bodies with physical exercise on a regular basis, we reduce our risk of cardiovascular disease, maintain our weight, improve our mood, and boost our energy level. Physical exercise can also change our bodies. We strengthen our muscles and bones, we lose fat, and we improve our lung capacity. When we train our brains on a regular basis with the practice of mindfulness, we experience many of the same wellness benefits. Interestingly, many scientific studies over the past few decades have shown proof that the body and the mind are inseparable (Baime, 2011). Recent research on the effects of mindfulness have indicated a strong mindfulness practice can help us in more ways than we might think, both in our personal and professional worlds. A study conducted by Liddy and Good (2015) suggests that mindfulness positively impacts human functioning. It improves attention by helping us remain focused. It can also help improve cognition, emotions, and coping behaviors. Mindfulness has been shown to positively affect interpersonal relationships by helping us develop greater empathy and compassion for self and for others. Research also shows mindfulness helps strengthen our resilience, which allows us to "roll with the punches" (Riopel, 2020). Is it actually possible to "retrain" the brain? The brain is a very interesting and complex organ. It consists of trillions of synapses and neurons whose primary function is to help brain cells communicate with each other. The brain's job description includes controlling body temperature and regulating blood pressure, heart rate, and breathing. It processes information about the world around you using your senses, it controls your physical movement, and it allows you to experience emotions. The brain is also plastic, and this neuroplasticity means that the brain has the ability to learn, grow, and change by reorganizing its synaptic connections. So how does mindfulness affect changes in the brain?

Lutz et al. (2008) determined that the region of the brain, known as the amygdala, which is primarily associated with emotional processes, tends to be less active and have greater gray matter density when one practices the art of mindfulness. The hippocampus, which is the region of the brain associated with memory and which helps regulate the amygdala, was found to be more active when practicing mindfulness (Goldin & Gross, 2010). Another study by Chiesa and Serretti (2010) examined the prefrontal cortex, the region of the brain responsible for impulse control and maturity and found this part of the brain became more active as well with the practice of mindfulness. Treadway and Lazar (2009) found that practicing mindfulness increases activity in the anterior subdivision of the cingulate cortex. This area of the brain plays a key role in motivation, attention capacity, and motor control. A study led by Donald et al. (2016), found that practicing mindfulness helps facilitate an adaptive response to daily stressors and helps improve the regulation of emotions, leading to a better ability to handle anxiety (Remmers et al., 2016). In other words, the practice of mindfulness can cause structural changes in the brain which are beneficial in reducing stress and anxiety, improving focus and efficiency, and helping hardwire the brain to become less reactive and calmer. With mindfulness, you slowly regain balance, opening your mind to new perspectives and new possibilities.

Figure 4

Your Brain on Mindfulness!

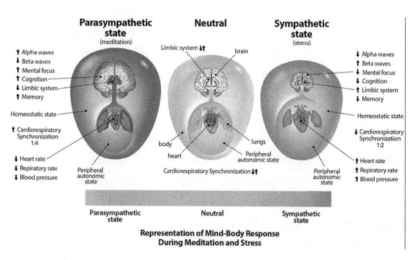

Note: Reprinted from Creative Commons—Open Access

Mindfulness Begins with the Breath (or the Lipstick)

Many people associate being mindful with the practice of meditation, and in some cases, these two terms are used interchangeably. Meditation is a mental exercise that helps to strengthen and improve the ability to focus attention and control emotions. Think of mindfulness as the underlying concept and meditation as a tool used to achieve it. Being mindful doesn't require practicing meditation, even though meditation has been shown to strengthen it. Mindfulness is the ability to have an open awareness of the present moment, free of judgement. It is a way to liberate yourself from dwelling on the past or worrying about the future. Mindfulness can bring about a sense of peace and tranquility, but it takes some effort to achieve. Let's start with the breath.

Mindfulness versus Meditation: Mindfulness is the underlying concept, and meditation is the tool used to achieve it.

The breath can teach us a lot about rhythm, pace, and steadfastness. Most of the time, we are not even aware of our breath. We breathe in and we breath out without much thought. At times, we can hold our breath or increase or decrease the rate of our breathing, but in the end, breathing is something we don't think much about. When we are faced with a fight-or-flight situation, our heart rate increases, our muscles tense, and our breathing may quicken, but when the threat is over, the breath is what encourages rest and recuperation. How many times, after a stressful situation has passed, have you muttered, "Just let me catch my breath"? Mindful breathing allows us to move away from a fast-paced, stress-inducing state into a restful, calm, and relaxed state.

The most basic way to perform mindful breathing is to simply focus on the inhale and the exhale. Taking deep, slow breaths helps us relax and focus. It is natural for the mind to wander but redirecting the mind to focus on breathing while avoiding self-criticism is what helps encourage success in the mindfulness practice. Once you have brought your consciousness into the process of breathing, you will be able to move your attention to the thoughts and feelings trying to lure your mind from the breath. Notice and acknowledge the thoughts and feelings, but don't get caught up in overthinking. Mindfulness, after all, is about awareness, not thinking (Harris, 2008). Awareness, along with an attitude of acceptance toward your thoughts and feelings, leads to a sense of peacefulness and calm, and this is what the art of mindfulness is all about. Mindfulness can help boost feelings of contentment and happiness, can strengthen relationships, and can even improve your physical health by decreasing stress and anxiety.

I once worked with a nurse who had a clever and unique way of redirecting her mind and controlling her breath during stressful situations. This nurse was an extraordinary CCU nurse and had a very colorful and bold personality. When a crisis or emergency arose on the unit, this particular nurse, before doing anything, would pull her lipstick out of her pocket and apply it. The first time I saw her do it, I thought it was a joke; I mean, after all, we were having a crisis on the unit. Why was applying lipstick important? However, after watching this same behavior occur over and over, I became curious. I finally found the courage to ask her why she applied her lipstick before taking action. Her response was simple: I stop, I pause, I breathe, then I act. The lipstick was her tool for keeping her mind focused and her anxiety at bay. She was able to confront the crisis in a calm, focused, and mindful manner, which had a ripple effect on the other team members. Never underestimate the power of the breath or of the lipstick.

Mindfulness Versus Multitasking: Truth be Told

If you take pride in being a strong multi-tasker, raise your hand! As frontline nursing staff, we can hang IV medications, assess urine output, survey the room for safety issues, and have a therapeutic conversation with our patient all at the same time. As nurse leaders, we can check emails, participate in a conference call, and plan a meeting agenda all while rounding on our staff. Nursing, by its very nature, involves multitasking, and many of us wear the ability to multitask as a badge of honor. At times, we relate our productivity, effectiveness, and even self-worth to our ability to multitask. Recent studies, however, have indicated that "multitasking" is not all that it is cracked up to be. Our brains are not nearly as good at handling multiple tasks at once as we would like to think they are. Powell (2016) suggests that multitasking lowers IQ, decreases productivity by

40%, and has been shown to shrink gray matter. The term "multitask" originated in the 1960s and was used to describe the computer's ability to process several tasks concurrently. Computers were designed to multitask; humans were not. Despite the belief that multitasking is the ability to accomplish multiple things at the same time, what multitasking really means is shifting attention from one thing to the next. Neuroscientists call this practice of rapidly switching between tasks "task switching." Most times this switching is done unconsciously, making it harder to focus. It can actually affect cognitive ability. Multitasking can lead to higher levels of stress, especially when the tasks are considered important or demanding. During these times, the brain pumps out adrenaline and other stress hormones, which, over time, can affect overall health and well-being. Ongoing stress impacts thinking and memory, leading to greater levels of anxiety. In other words, the art of multitasking and the art of mindfulness are polar opposites.

Being a Mindful Leader

What is mindful leadership? What does a mindful leader look like? What does mindfulness have to do with leadership excellence? According to John Maxwell, an American author and coach, "Leadership is not about titles, positions, or flowcharts. It is about one life influencing another." Leaders, whether they be at the bedside or in the boardroom, have a ripple effect on those around them. In her book *Finding the Space to Lead: A Practical Guide to Mindful Leadership,* Janice Marturano (2015), founder and executive director of the Institute for Mindful Leadership, describes a mindful leader as someone who embodies leadership presence through focus, clarity, creativity, and compassion in the service of others. *Focus* allows the leader to sustain their attention, without distraction, on the problems at hand. *Clarity* allows the leader to see things as they are, not as they would like or hope them to be. It involves not only seeing our environment around us in a clearer way, it also includes seeing ourselves more clearly. *Creativity* requires space, and practicing mindfulness allows us to create mental space that is clear of wandering thoughts and interruptions. Finally, *compassion* reminds us that we are part of a larger picture and we all share a common humanity.

Marturano describes mindful leadership as having the tangible quality of leadership presence. Leadership presence, she says, requires "full and complete non-judgmental attention in the present moment. Those around a mindful leader see and feel that presence" (p. 11). Several years ago, I was interviewing for a position at a large urban hospital. One of my interviews included spending time with the chief nursing officer (CNO). I remember walking into her office. She stepped away from her desk, greeting me with a smile and a handshake. She pulled two chairs together, and we sat down to begin the interview. What I remember most is her taking out her phone and turning it off. She looked me in the eye and told me that she wanted some uninterrupted time in which to get to know me. We spent over an hour talking, laughing, and just getting to know each other. She was present. She wasn't rushed or distracted. She wasn't worried about yesterday and wasn't dreading tomorrow (at least that was the impression I got). The interview was one of my best experiences, not because I interviewed all that well, but because I remember the way I felt. I had the CNO's attention, our conversation was intentional, and we connected. The CNO was curious, focused, and non-judgmental. After the interview, I couldn't wait to begin my new role. I learned many "small" lessons during the interview that helped shape the way I would lead my team. I learned that mindful and meaningful communication is a deliberate practice. It is about removing the distractions, keeping your mind focused on the present, and being an active participant, both as a listener and a communicator. As a Human-Centered Leader, doing anything less is disrespectful.

Embracing the art of mindfulness allows you to be totally present in the moment with focus, clarity, creativity, and non-judgement. As a nurse leader, mindful presence is a powerful and effective human skill. Mindfulness, at its core, is the building block for developing a strong sense of self-awareness. When a leader is confident and comfortable with who they are, others around them also feel confident and comfortable. Being present in the moment with someone, void of distractions or interruptions, shows a true sense of caring and empathy for that person, often inspiring them towards individual success. Marturano calls this the "ripple effect" and points out that having the ability to embody leadership presence is critical as a leader but also affects those around us. When a leader is authentically present and engaged, the ripple effect is very different from when a leader is distracted or disengaged. Marturano reminds us that it isn't enough to want to be present or to want to have a positive ripple effect within the work environment, we have to commit to training our brains. As Maya Angelou reminded us, "People will forget what you said, people will forget what you did, but people will never forget how you made them feel." Never underestimate the power of mindfulness.

DISCUSSION QUESTIONS

1. What does mindful leadership look like to you?
2. Describe a situation where your leader was engaged and present. How did you feel? Did you experience a ripple effect?
3. Describe a situation where your leader was distracted and disengaged. How did you feel?
4. What happens when we move from "I" to the "we" of mindfulness?

REFLECTION

What are some ways that I can become a more mindful and present leader? What does being a more mindful and present leader do to influence the culture of the work environment?

_____

_____

_____

_____

_____

_____

REFERENCES

Angell, G. (2017, October 20). *A story about living in the present moment.* www.gregoryangell.com/2017/10

Baime, M. (2011, July). *This is your brain on mindfulness.* http://www.uphs.upenn.edu/pastoral/events/Baime_SHAMBHALA_2011.pdf

Chiesa, A., & Serretti, A. (2010). A systematic review of neurobiological and clinical features of mindfulness meditations. *Psychological Medicine*, 40(08), 1239–1252.

Davin, S. (2017, October 25). *Evidence-based mindfulness: What science tells us about mindfulness meditation and its benefits*. Cleveland Clinic. https://consultqd.clevelandclinic.org/evidence-based-mindfulness-what-science-tells-us-about-mindfulness-meditation-and-its-benefits/

Donald, J. N., Atkins, P. W. B, Parker, P. D. Christie, A. M. & Tyan, R. M. (2016). Daily stress and the benefits of mindfulness: Examining the daily and longitudinal relations between present moment awareness and stress responses. *Journal of Research in Personality*, 65, 30–37.

Goldin, P. R., & Gross, J. J. (2010). Effects of mindfulness-based stress reduction. (MBSR) on emotion regulation in social anxiety disorder. *Emotion*, 10(1), 83.

Good, D. J., Lyddy, C. J., Glomb, T. M., Bono, J. E., Brown, K. W., Duffy, M. K., Baer, R. A., Brewer, J. A., & Lazar, S. W. (2015). Contemplating mindfulness at work: An integrative review. *Journal of Management*, 42(1), 114–142.

Harris, R. (2008). *The happiness trap: How to stop struggling and start living.* Trumpeter Books, Exisle Publishing LTD. Australia.

Lutz. A., Slagter, H. A., Dunne, J. D., & Davidson, R. J. (2008). Attention regulation and monitoring in meditation. *Trends in Cognitive Sciences*, 12(4), 163–169.

Marturano, J. (2015). *Finding the space to lead: A practical guide to mindful leadership.* Bloomsbury Press.

Mindful. (2017, January 11). "Jon Kabat-Zinn: Defining Mindfulness." https://www.mindful.org/jon-kabat-zinn-defining-mindfulness/

Powell, S. K. (2016, March/April). Mindfulness multitasking and you. *Professional Case Management*, 21(2), 61–62.

Remmers, C. Topolinski, S., & Koole, S. C. (2016). Why being mindful may have more benefits than you realize: Mindfulness improves both explicit and implicit mood regulation. *Mindfulness*, 7 827–829.

Riopel, L. (2020, November 9). *Mindfulness and the brain: What does research and neuroscience say?* Positive Psychology. https://positivepsychology.com/mindfulness-brain-research-neuroscience/

Roy, S. (n.d.). *Mindfulness in 7 steps: An easy guide to practice mindfulness.* https://happyproject.in/mindfulness-7-steps/

Treadway, M. T., & Lazar, S. W. (2009). The neurobiology of mindfulness. In Didonna, F. (Ed.) *Clinical Handbook of Mindfulness* (pp. 45-5). Springer.

Zack, D. (2015). *Singletasking: Get more done-one thing at a time.* The Single task Sensation the Costoo Connection P.13

RECOMMENDED READING

Chiesa, A., & Serretti, A. (2010). A systematic review of neurobiological and clinical features of mindfulness meditations. *Psychological Medicine*, 40(08), 1239-1252.

Goldin, P. R., & Gross, J. J. (2010). Effects of mindfulness-based stress reduction. (MBSR) on emotion regulation in social anxiety disorder. *Emotion*, 10(1), 83.

Lutz. A., Slagter, H. A. Dunne, J. D., & Davidson, R. J. (2008). Attention regulation and monitoring in meditation. *Trends in Cognitive Sciences*, 12(4), 163–169.

Marchant, J. (2016) *Cure: A journey into the science of mind over body.* Broadway Books.

Marturano, J. (2015). Finding the space to lead: A practical guide to mindful leadership. Bloomsbury Press.

Remmers, C., Topolinski, S., & Koole, S. C. (2016). Why being mindful may have more benefits than you realize: Mindfulness improves both explicit and implicit mood regulation. *Mindfulness*, 7, 827–829.

Scott, S. J., & Davenport, B. (2016) *Declutter you mind: How to stop worrying, relieve anxiety, and eliminate negative thinking.* Oldtown Publishing.

PART III
It's Not About You

The Human-Centered Leader focuses their leadership outward by integrating the leadership attributes of the Upholder, the Awakener, and the Connector.

Chapter 6

But It's Not About You!

"Leadership is service, not position."
—**Tim Fargo**, American Author, Entrepreneur, and Writer

Have you noticed the number of personality tests seem to be expanding? I first found out that I'm an ENFJ on the Myers-Briggs personality assessment (Myers-Briggs, n.d.); then I learned I'm a collaborator and creator on the Competing Values Framework Model (Cameron & Quinn, n.d.). I'm an "I" on the DISC Personality Assessment Tool (Harris & Guy, 2020), and now I'm an Enneagram Type 2 with a Type 3 Wing (Enneagram Personality Test, 2020). So…who am I?

When it comes to Human-Centered Leadership in Healthcare, rest assured you won't be categorized as an Awakener, a Connector, or an Upholder. These others-oriented leadership attributes are interconnected and together create the culture change in healthcare that results in sustained outcomes. It's similar to the idea of well-being. To have a balanced and healthy life, you must focus on mind, body, and spirit since wellness in all three is necessary. The same is true for a Human-Centered Leader. You need to develop each aspect of others-focused leadership—the Awakener, the Connector, and the Upholder—in order to create and sustain a healthy culture. If the only required outcomes in healthcare were patient experience and staff satisfaction, then perhaps you could focus only on the attributes of the Upholder. But what about the required outcomes of quality care, patient safety, team collaboration, population health, connection with the community—the list goes on. Obviously, the organization would not be able to survive, much less thrive, without a focus on all the many metrics that indicate value to the patient, the staff, the community, and the payors. It takes all the attributes of Human-Centered Leadership to achieve all these results.

When you take the self-assessment for Human-Centered Leadership (Refer to Appendix A), you may learn that you have a natural tendency towards being an Awakener, for example, but need to develop the attributes of the Connector and the Upholder. As you learn more about the attributes, and about yourself, you will be guided toward strategies to build your ability to embody all three.

Personal well-being requires a balance of mind, body, and spirit. Similarly, the Human-Centered Leader requires a balance of the attributes of the Awakener, the Connector, and the Upholder.

In the story below, you will see how a Human-Centered Leader exemplifies the attributes of the Awakener, the Connector, and the Upholder. Because of the inherent complexity in healthcare, the interconnected leadership attributes produce a culture reflective of well-being in healthcare.

Exemplar

A surgical unit began to notice a slight uptick in the number of patient falls over a three-month period. During the unit's daily safety huddle, the nurse manager, Jamal, suggested the team investigate the cause of the increase and worked with the charge nurse to develop a unit-specific audit tool. Each day, the charge nurse assigned a staff nurse to perform the audit, and that nurse reported results during the safety huddle. The data was posted daily and areas for improvement were identified by the team. The safety issue was then presented to the nursing professional governance (NPG) council. During this meeting, a "falls champion" was identified for each shift. The falls champions met with Jamal to review the current audit tool, to identify additional contributing factors, and to begin a more thorough investigation of patient falls. Over the next several weeks, the falls champions, along with the charge nurse and Jamal, performed audits on every patient to determine if fall risk protocols were consistently in place for high-risk patients. The audits also included checking each patient bed to ensure the bed alarms were functioning properly. With daily reports at each safety huddle, the topic of patient falls became a shift-to-shift discussion among the team members. A team goal included 100% compliance with the high-risk fall protocol, however, during the audits the team discovered issues with non-functioning bed alarms. Jamal arranged for the engineering team to meet with the falls champions, and together they reviewed the audit of the beds and the bed alarm system. They noted that many of the bed alarm cords were not plugged into the wall because the small prongs inside the plugs were broken. The engineering team took inventory and replaced all broken cords. The falls champions began to reeducate the nursing team on the bed alarm system. The nurses identified the patient transport team as a group also requiring reeducation. Jamal worked with the falls champions to schedule educational sessions for the patient transport team. Continued audits for one month after the education sessions revealed no reported patient falls or near misses. The falls champions continued to audit and educate as needed. Over the next six-month period, there were no patient falls. Jamal planned a celebration for the unit to acknowledge their hard work and their successful result on this patient safety issue. Jamal also suggested that the falls champions submit their work as a best practice poster presentation at a local nursing conference. He reached out to the unit educator to serve as a mentor and coach for the two nurses who had served as falls champions. The nurses submitted their poster and were awarded second place for an innovative best practice.

Embodying an *Awakener*: Motivator, Mentor, Coach, Architect, and Advocate

Jamal recognized the problem with patient falls and quickly went to work engaging and **mentoring** the team. His initial step, working with the charge nurse to develop an audit tool, exemplified the importance of including the leaders and nurses closest to the point of care to develop the solutions. The audit, performed by a unit nurse, was shared each day at the safety huddle, allowing the care team to own the data and use it as the basis for their learning. This real-time feedback enhanced the staff's connection to their purpose—to deliver high quality and safe patient care (**motivator**).

The responsibility for the solution was handed off to the NPG council, the structure Jamal had built on the unit for point-of-care decision-making (**architect**). Also, a falls champion for each shift was elected, further enlarging the influence of the team. Jamal worked with the falls champions to tweak the audit tool based on their new knowledge and provided **coaching** on the improvement process.

Jamal **advocated** for the team by engaging the engineering department to work with the falls champions and remedy the technical problem related to the bed alarms. This problem with the bed alarms would likely not have been uncovered had Jamal gone about the process improvement in a different way. Imagine if he had blamed the staff for being inattentive to their patients and being careless about using bed alarms. The staff would have possibly become disengaged and silent, and the engineering department would not have known a problem existed.

Lastly, Jamal recognized the staff for the solution by celebrating their success. He cleared the path for them to move forward with a poster presentation and ensured further **mentoring** and **coaching** by the unit educator. His actions contributed to the culture of excellence because he was comfortable being the Awakener, rather than the hero!

Embodying a *Connector*: Collaborator, Supporter, Edgewalker, Engineer, Authentic Communicator

Jamal understood that as a Connector, his main goal was to unify the team around the organization's mission, vision, and values. He demonstrated

authentic communication with the team as he gathered them for the safety huddle each day. He used open, honest communication to demonstrate his trust and respect for the team.

When the uptick in patient falls was noted, Jamal didn't overreact to the data by quickly putting a new initiative in place for the team to follow. A traditional leader might have instituted a falls checklist to be used by every nurse with every patient interaction and then monitored the team for compliance. Instead, Jamal seemed to embrace the problem as an opportunity for the team to innovate and problem-solve. By recognizing that problems are inevitable and embracing uncertainty as an opportunity for innovation, Jamal demonstrated the fine art of **edgewalking**. He knew how to hold the precise tension between essential processes while also being open to new learning, surprises, and innovation.

Jamal **supported** the findings of the NPG council and welcomed the opportunity for the staff to **collaborate** with the transport team on a shared goal. He knew that by engaging the falls champions in the process and using the skill of the unit educator, the solution would likely be more sustainable (**engineer**). Jamal's leadership behaviors contributed to a culture of trust because he trusted the wisdom of the team and connected both people and processes to develop a solution.

Embodying an *Upholder:* Personally Well, Mindful, Others-Oriented, Emotionally Aware, and Socially and Organizationally Aware

Jamal exemplified Human-Centered Leadership by first recognizing that he didn't have all the answers. He was vulnerable with the team, recognizing them as the influencers and problem-solvers (**others-oriented**). He could have piled this responsibility on top of his already busy schedule, and possibly overreacted due to the additional stress. Instead, he remained calm and present, likely able to attend to his own self-care (**personally well**). Through **emotional awareness** and **mindfulness**, he embedded himself within the team and demonstrated his trust and belief in their good intentions. There was no mention of blame or shame. Jamal's actions demonstrated he was concerned about the patients on the unit, rather the uptick in the data and the reflection the data could have on him as the leader (**others-oriented**).

Lastly, Jamal was **socially and organizationally aware**. He knew how to collaborate with others outside the unit, e.g. the engineering department and the patient transporters, without placing blame. He demonstrated his ability to navigate organizational politics and bring people together around shared purpose. By demonstrating the attributes of the Upholder, Jamal contributed to a culture of caring that likely impacted the satisfaction of both the caregivers and their patients.

In the next three chapters, we'll take a deep dive into the three sets of attributes of the Human-Centered Leader. You'll learn more about the Awakener, the Connector, and the Upholder so you can better incorporate the attributes into your leadership approach and become the leader that your team will follow to the end of the earth.

DISCUSSION QUESTIONS

1. Do you have a strong NPG council in place to refer a patient care problem, such as an increase in "never" events? If not, what are your next steps in developing this structure?

2. As a leader, you have likely encountered an increase in a "never" event. How did you handle it? Does Jamal's story highlight any areas of leadership you could consider including?

3. Consider the best practices provided in the exemplar. How can you share best practices across your organization and still maintain staff ownership?

REFLECTION

Think about the current culture of your unit or department. Does the culture reflect excellence, trust, and caring? Which area needs your attention and why?

_____

_____

_____

_____

_____

_____

REFERENCES

Cameron, K., & Quinn, R. (n.d.). *The Competing Values Culture Assessment.* Competing Values Product Line. https://www.boomhogeronderwijs.nl/media/8/download_pdf_culture_assessment_workbook.pdf

Harris, G., & Eikenberry, K. (2020). *DISC Personality Test.* DISC Personality Testing. https://discpersonalitytesting.com/free-disc-test/

The Myers-Briggs Company. (n.d.) *Myers-Briggs Type Indicator.* https://www.themyersbriggs.com/en-US/Products-and-Services/Myers-Briggs

Truity. (2020). *Emmeagram Personality Test.* (2020). https://www.truity.com/test/enneagram-personality-test

RECOMMENDED READING

Kennedy, K., Campis, S., & Leclerc, L. (2020). Human-centered leadership in health care: Creating change from the inside out. *Nurse Leader*, 18(3), 227–231.

Chapter 7

The Awakener: Developing a Culture of Excellence

"I am not a teacher but an awakener."
—**Robert Frost**, American Poet

There are those leaders, in academia or in practice, who are particularly strong in the attributes of the Awakener because of their focus on education. I want to share a story about a clinical nurse specialist who definitively embodied the attributes of the Awakener as a way of highlighting and examining each attribute more closely. I hope this story causes you to think about leaders in your journey who knew how to reveal the excellence that already existed within each team member.

Exemplar

As the director of critical care services, I had the honor of working with a clinical nurse specialist, Jackie, who was an expert in critical care. She was passionate about sharing her knowledge of critical care nursing with bedside staff in a way that made the science of caring for the critically ill come to life. The nurses entrusted to Jackie's teaching felt honored and "special" to be her students and wore that sense of belonging and accomplishment as a badge. Jackie held a high bar for participation in education and established a culture where expertise was expected, authentic care for the patient was essential, and continued growth strengthened the nurses' purpose and belonging. Her passion for excellence overflowed in each interaction and she exemplified the saying that "knowledge is power." Despite her "power," she demonstrated the upmost humility and respect for everyone on the team.

Jackie developed the orientation program to prepare surgical/trauma intensive care nurses to advance their learning and become the expert staff needed to care for patients undergoing cardiac surgery. This was a new program added at a large public hospital to complete the cardiac service line. The orientation program was rigorous and included learning to read EKG strips, recognize ST-elevation myocardial infarctions (STEMIs), provide acute and post-acute care of STEMI patients, and provide post-op care to cardiac surgery patients. The nurses who took on this additional workload and training were internally motivated by the desire to become better, and frankly to become more like Jackie. Since Jackie was well established as an expert in critical care, she modeled the expertise and leadership that the best of the best ICU nurses wanted to emulate.

The nurses in this program owned their development and worked as a team to provide the support needed for the overall program. They mapped out a schedule to be sure at least one of them was slated to work in the ICU each shift. They did this to ensure the level of care for cardiac patients would be optimal, should a patient require it. The other nurses on the unit, who were not a part of the advanced cohort, equally shared in the collaboration as they supported their "cardiac" teammates.

The cardiac cohort of nurses spent hours in the classroom, studied and reviewed EKGs, and took comprehension and applicability tests. Because of their personal investment, they owned their outcomes and were committed to the success of the program. Along with their commitment came the confidence and empowerment to freely bring forward concerns and disagreements with surgeons and other members of the healthcare team if it meant they could together improve trust and communication. The authentic communication and productive conflict around different perspectives pushed the team to become better and made the program a huge success.

As a result of their ownership in the program and their desire to make it as comprehensive as possible, the team self-organized, with Jackie's oversight, into a chest pain evaluation team. They wanted to be sure that inpatients who had symptoms of cardiac ischemia had access to the same rapid diagnosis and treatment as patients admitted through the emergency department. The Rapid Response Team, traditionally the team who responds to patients in cardiac arrest, were educated on the process and together the expanded nurse team began responding to in-house episodes of chest pain. The nurses were successful as first responders in their assessment of patients, collaboration with the cardiologists, and ability to move the patient through the algorithm for prompt diagnosis and treatment. Jackie was, of course, right there with them—one of the team.

As the program progressed, one of the surgeons had the idea of standardizing the handoff at the bedside from cardiac surgery to critical care. The cardiac nurses took the lead and established the handoff process from the cardiac surgery operating room team to the critical care team of physicians, nurses, and other disciplines. When a patient arrived in the ICU after cardiac surgery, the interprofessional team gathered at the bedside for a thorough hand-off on the patient's care. As you may have guessed, the cardiac nurses lead the hand-off and ensured that the prescribed process was consistently followed.

Leaders like Jackie, natural Awakeners, stir the excellence that already exists in their team. Jackie's leadership ignited the team's desire to grow because she modeled continuous learning, invested in each staff member, set a high bar for engagement, and created a learning environment. Jackie and the nurses celebrated every learning milestone and patient success, which, along with their sense of self-accomplishment, provided the fuel needed to keep the team highly engaged.

While this story is about an exceptional clinical leader, all Human-Centered Leaders, with differing levels of expertise, can model the characteristics of an Awakener. As an Awakener, you set the expectation for continuous learning and infuse it in clinical practice through collaboration with clinical experts. I mentioned that Jackie was an extremely humble leader who worked hard to keep her collaborative relationships strong. She credited the team with every success.

An Awakener never takes on the attitude of the "hero" but instead elevates those on the team who have worked to deserve the respect associated with excellence.

Quality programs in healthcare typically refer to "loop closure" as a way to continuously study and improve processes related to patient care. This hospital accomplished loop closure for the cardiac service line by studying each case as a collaborative team. The team included emergency medical services (EMS), cardiologists, nursing leaders, a cardiac catheterization lab team member, and a quality expert. When at all possible, one of the staff nurses from the cardiac cohort attended as well. The team tried to learn from each case and then implemented changes based on their new knowledge. This is what true accountability looks like.

It's easy to see the impact of the Awakener through Jackie's story. Again, the purpose of this story is to help you better understand the attributes of an Awakener so you can work to develop them in your leadership practice. The payoff comes as your behaviors impact both the staff and the environment. You don't need to become the world-renowned expert in your clinical area, but you do need to set the expectation of growth and development and create a learning environment as you collaborate with clinical experts. When you embrace the attributes of the Awakener, you'll see that the team owns their individual and collaborative practice and implements innovative solutions based on their new knowledge (Leclerc et al., 2020a). In short, keep your sights on "awakening" excellence in each staff member. By embracing the attributes of the Awakener, your team will achieve market-leading outcomes and the ultimate success will be realized by the patient who receives the highest quality care. If one of my family members requires cardiac care, I would not hesitate to take them to the hospital described earlier. I know, firsthand, that the nursing care there is excellent.

Who is the Awakener?

As you become comfortable with the attributes of the Awakener, keep in mind that your goal is to ignite the desire within each team member to learn, grow, and become the best they can be. This requires you to take a genuine interest in those on the team and believe that they are capable of more than they realize. Think about a time when a respected leader or teacher believed in you and encouraged you to do more than you thought possible. It's a humbling and empowering experience to receive this type of validation. Think about the ripples of excellence that can result from this type of leadership. It starts with your focus inward, being comfortable with vulnerability, practicing continuous growth, and modeling a purposeful career and meaningful life.

Table 2

Defined Attributes Embodied by the Human-Centered Leader as an Awakener

Awakener	Cultivates our people
Motivator	Establishes a learning culture with high expectations for ongoing learning for self and others
Coach	Provides honest feedback, address behaviors inconsistent with learning culture
Mentor	Advises on member accountability for individual growth plans
Architect	Designs structures/processes so innovation can emerge
Advocate	Ensures resources are available for best practice and professional growth

Note: Adapted from Leclerc, L., Kennedy, K., & Campis, S. (2020). Human-centered leadership in healthcare: An idea that's time has come. *Nursing Administration Quarterly, 44*(2), 117-126 and Leclerc, L., Kennedy, K., & Campis, S. (2021). Human-centered leadership in healthcare: A contemporary nursing leadership theory generated via constructivist grounded theory. *Journal of Nursing Management, 29*, 294–306.

The attributes of the Awakener are: motivator, mentor, coach, architect, and advocate (Refer to Table 2). As you learn more about these attributes in the sections below, notice the direct quotes the nurses in our research used when describing their experiences with the leaders they valued most along their journey (Refer to Table 3).

Motivator

As leaders, we know that you cannot force someone to become motivated. Motivation comes from within. You can, however, help connect personal and professional growth opportunities with the individual staff member's goals and

Figure 5

The Awakener

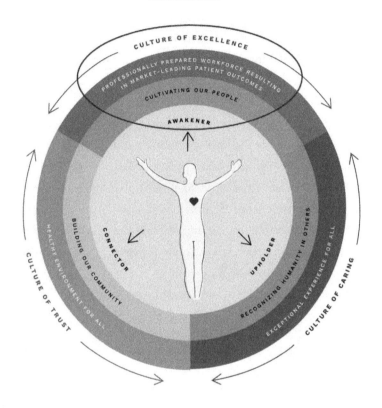

Note: Adapted Leclerc, L., Kennedy, K., & Campis, S. (2020). Human-centered leadership in healthcare: An idea that's time has come. *Nursing Administration Quarterly, 44*(2), 117-126.

sense of purpose. As you get to know each team member, seek to understand their goals and "look for opportunities" to connect them to their goals and purpose. This is a key step in awakening excellence within individuals.

You will learn that establishing a learning environment is motivating to your team. When problem-solving, there should be multidirectional dialogue with the staff rather than one-way communication from you to the staff. If you provide a definitive linear process to achieve a goal, the team has little ownership in the process or the results. You will find yourself monitoring the process and becoming frustrated with the team's lack of motivation to comply. If you instead develop a learning environment and allow the team to experiment, based on their experience and researched best practices, they are motivated to develop processes that work for them and meet the desired outcomes. A learning environment connects the staff to their internal motivation to grow professionally and provide the best care for their patients.

As you focus on learning, don't hesitate to hold a high, but reachable, bar for continued growth. Clearly communicate that the high bar stems from a passionate desire to provide the upmost expertise and the highest quality of care for patients. Setting the high bar also reflects your belief in the team's capabilities. Unless the bar is a stretch, requiring a significant investment, accomplishing the goals won't carry the same sense of pride that develops into a motivating passion. In Jackie's case, she had to eliminate nurses from the cohort if they didn't meet the rigorous expectations. There's no trophy for being a passive member of the team. Jackie required a substantial investment in the work, knowing this would gain the most valuable dividends for the team members.

As your team members feel motivated and empowered by their learning, there is an infectious spread to others. Nurses own their professional growth to ensure their expertise and confidence in providing exceptional care to their patients. Ultimately, this provides a way for the nurses to connect to and sustain their purpose—making a difference in the lives of patients by providing high-quality patient care.

To further connect to staff members' internal motivation, encourage each member to develop an individual professional growth plan to help them stay connected to continued growth and purpose (Refer to Table 4). This plan should be reviewed as a part of their annual employee performance appraisal. The employee owns their growth plan, and your role is to encourage, mentor, support, and advocate for each of them as they work through their plan. The nurses in our research referred to this as "extending ownership for growth while offering support." Those not interested in meeting the challenge to grow professionally will typically self-select out of the unit because their lack of engagement will set them apart from the team.

Motivator in Action: A new nurse begins work on a medical-surgical unit, and you learn from your conversation with him that his ultimate goal is to provide global nursing care to underserved populations through a nonprofit organization. He wants to learn as much as possible about medical-surgical nursing in preparation for an autonomous practice. Your role as a motivator is to tie his professional goals to those of the unit by seeking out opportunities that will build his knowledge, confidence, and expertise. You might also look for opportunities for him to be a member of a problem-solving team and eventually a team leader. Together, discuss what success will look like for him and what steps are needed to get there.

Mentor

As you develop the attributes of the Awakener, you will recognize the value of becoming a mentor. The nurses in our research felt that a mentor "promotes growth" for individuals and "builds the team." As a mentor, you will become a model for others because you possess the required professional skills and even more importantly, you live your personal values. Our nurse participants listed "honesty," "transparency," "trust," "communication," "appropriate flexibility," "self-development," and "self-care" as valuable characteristics of a mentor. Mentors are in the business of developing other leaders, so as a mentor, you will interpret and model the characteristics and role of the leader to others.

As you mentor your staff, especially those new to their careers, you will expose them to different, challenging situations. If they are to build on important steps and missteps, you must allow room for learning and for inevitable errors. This will require foresight, flexibility, and patience. As a mentor, you need to clear the path to make these opportunities available at the right time to the right team members. As your relationship develops and you learn of specific behaviors they are trying to develop, the relationship can evolve into one-to-one coaching.

Mentor in Action: You are the manager of a medical-surgical unit, and a relatively new nurse on the unit lets you know that she would like to become a charge nurse. You know she's not ready yet, but as a mentor, you look for ways to expose her to different aspects of the position. You have her work with a seasoned charge nurse to develop competencies such as leading huddles, making assignments, and ensuring patient flow. Your organization has access to a leadership program to help develop new leaders, so you provide this opportunity as well. You also encourage other nurses working on the transition to charge nurse to become peer coaches for each other. Over time, the staff nurse will learn and grow from her own mistakes, and you will learn where further coaching would be helpful in achieving her goal of becoming a charge nurse.

Coach

As you develop your skills as a coach, you'll recognize the significance of honest and thoughtful feedback to further each team member's growth. Often feedback is best received in the form of a question, born out of curiosity, which allows the nurse to discover the answer for themself. The intent of feedback is to improve practice and to reveal blind spots that may stem from years of habit or a lack of awareness. Through thoughtful and sensitive coaching, you will bring blind spots into the light, discuss opportunities for change, and look for progress rather than perfection. Through direct and honest feedback, you must acknowledge the humanity of each individual and establish an environment where team members can focus on specific areas for improvement. As a coach, you are conscious of not telling the team member what to do, which could be interpreted as micromanaging. Instead, you help the individual staff member determine appropriate next steps and encourage movement towards progress. Since the Human-Centered Leader understands the work and the perspective of the staff members, the feedback, delivered in a sensitive manner, will likely be well received. As a coach, you will expect mistakes and setbacks. Use these as opportunities for further learning through the practice of reflection.

Coach in Action: Consider the medical-surgical nurse in the previous story who wanted to become a charge nurse. As a mentor, you've ensured she was exposed to the tasks required of a charge nurse, participated in peer coaching, and completed a self-directed leadership course. She lets you know the area she needs to develop is assigning new admissions to team members. She states that she lacks confidence in her decisions. As a coach, ask about her biggest concern and what she thinks would give her more confidence in her ability to make sound decisions in this area. It may be that she needs practice walking through the process in real time. Discuss possible solutions such as working through the decision with other charge nurses or working through the decision with a peer coach. You don't always have to be the coach yourself, but you must ensure that the staff member receives the coaching they need to progress forward. Remember that everyone needs a coach; it's not a sign of weakness but a sign of initiative and motivation.

Architect

Let's go back for a moment to consider the earlier analogy of the downtown hospital under construction. As you grow in the attributes of the Awakener, you will function as an architect and will build the invisible infrastructure that supports the team. The infrastructure includes core values that are lived every day such as respect, commitment to self, commitment to the team, and dedication to expertise in patient care (Tye & Dent, 2017). In addition, the infrastructure includes an NPG council, operational processes, and interconnections with multidisciplinary professionals. These components support the work of the team and the team's ability to achieve a culture of excellence.

The nurses in our research stated that their most admired leaders were able to develop and communicate a vision. They were able to "see a way forward" and "communicate to the team how to get there." A vision co-created by the nurses and the leader contributes further to the infrastructure of the unit and has the fingerprints of the team all over it. As a Human-Centered Leader, the plan for "how to get there" is developed *with* the team's input and ownership so the leader is not the sole owner but the team working together through the supportive structures creates the vision for moving forward.

In today's complex environment, with ever-growing financial constraints, you will need to be creative and leverage resources to provide ample time for nurses to work together in problem-solving teams. NPGs may look different than they did in the past. Decision-making might need to take place during brief huddles rather than in separate meetings. Either way, decision-making at the point of care must continue to exist and evolve. The interconnectedness of the team within and outside the unit, supported by the invisible infrastructure, is the key to influencing positive change throughout the organization.

Architect in Action: As you consider the attributes of the architect, assess the current core values, decision-making structure, policies, and interconnections across the unit and hospital. Even though we refer to these as the *invisible* infrastructure, they should be very clear components to you and the team members. This infrastructure supports the way you do things on the unit and in the organization and incorporates the vision for achieving excellence. You may find it helpful to ask new team members about their perception of the infrastructure to be sure that you and the team are making the invisible visible.

Advocate

Lastly, our research confirmed that being an Awakener means serving as an advocate. As an advocate, you will act as a resource, and when necessary, connect team members with other knowledgeable individuals. According to one of the nurses from our research, "If they don't know the answer, they know where to go to find the answer." As an advocate, you'll represent the team, and because of your position embedded in the work, you'll better understand the perspective of the team. By advocating for the team, it will be clear your intention is to facilitate an environment that breeds empowerment among the nurses.

The tools and ability to research best practices around point-of-care concerns are resources your team will need. They will also need to know how to adjust best practices to fit the organization. This will be your opportunity to ensure there are members on the team with research experience and that the resources are available to them. Once this is established, you can further advocate for the team to not only act on best practices but to begin adding to and improving best practices. Dr. Tim Porter-O'Grady and Dr. Kathy Malloch (2018) refer to this as recognizing evidence-based practice to be the "floor," or the starting point for clinical practice. Additional creativity and innovation, developed through NPG councils, allow the team to advance their clinical practice further, to the "ceiling." Skilled professional nurses working together in a learning environment can accomplish this type of advancement (Porter-O'Grady & Malloch, 2018; American Organization of Nurse Executives, 2015).

As you share your team's innovative solutions and practice changes across the organization, there will be a need for continued support and advocacy as solutions are adopted and changes are put in place. Measures of success must be established for all collaborating teams to bring about shared ownership. We will cover more about the process of change management in Chapter 11.

———————————

Advocate in Action: As a nurse manager during the COVID-19 pandemic, you and your team are aware that a second surge after the Thanksgiving holiday is approaching. You know that your team is becoming overly exhausted. Team members who are usually upbeat and positive have become negative, seemingly lacking the motivation to push through. The call-out rate has increased, and you struggle to staff the unit appropriately. You schedule an appointment with your director, who is also a Human-Centered Leader, to discuss the additional resources the team needs during this challenging time. Together you develop a plan to provide for mental health care through individual and group sessions with the mental health team. You brainstorm ways to support the team with additional staff and consider a different model of care. You discuss personal stressors that add to the team's concerns and develop a plan to seek input to determine what resources would be helpful. Your advocacy ensures the CNO is aware of specific needs and together you commit to resolve them to the best of your ability.

Table 3

Qualitative Research Connecting Participant Feedback
with Concepts and Attributes of the Awakener

Awakener: Cultivating our People → Culture of Excellence		
Category/Concept	**Participant Comments and In Vivo Codes**	**Attribute**
Supports Growth & Development	"Need leaders who want you to grow" Extends ownership of growth along with support Promotes growth and building the team	Advocate Motivator Mentor
Mentor/Coach	Knowledgeable about leadership roles Can mentor new leaders effectively Can help others understand the leadership role Flexible but needs to know where the line needs to be drawn" "flexible versus not knowing when to be flexible"	Coach Mentor
Visionary	Have a vision in order to know where the team is going Develop an understanding of how to achieve team goals Uses good communication skills to get the team on board Sees opportunity in everything	Architect Motivator

Leads by Example	Multiple mentions of leading by example regarding work/life balance, relationships, skills as a leader, skills as a nurse, honesty, transparency, trust, communication, development, self-care Nurse's nurse "Walk the walk" "I do what you do" Resource to the team Knowledgeable/competent	Coach Mentor Advocate
Team Player	Willingness to be "out there"—side by side with staff No separation between co-worker and boss Has a transformational style of leadership and understands that good leadership involves a "give and take" mentality Collaborator—"I'm a nurse with more paperwork" Symbiotic	Advocate
Knowledgeable/ Competent	Need to be able to do what they ask nurses to do Act as a resource—"if you don't know the answer, you know where to go to find the answer" "When leader speaks on behalf of the staff, they need to have the knowledge base and competency level to speak intelligently… knowing what the nurses do"	Coach Mentor Advocate

Note: From Leclerc, Kennedy, and Campis (2021) Human-centered leadership in healthcare: A contemporary nursing leadership theory generated via constructivist grounded theory. *Journal of Nursing Management*. 29, 294–306.

The Awakener Meets Complexity

Porter-O'Grady and Malloch (2018), experts in complexity science and leadership, state that "aligning staff motivation with organizational goals is the only sustainable way of ensuring staff investment and ownership" (p. 147). Since we know that true motivation comes from within, you inspire motivation in individuals by aligning their inner desires with the work of the organization. This requires you to coach and mentor individuals rather than direct them and to delegate opportunities that will help individuals to grow. It is through your coaching and mentoring, the team's work through NPG councils, and your advocacy that rich relationships are formed, and people self-organize and adapt to change. You, as an Awakener, encourage creativity and innovation by embracing the team's learning and any innovative surprises that emerge.

Outcomes Resulting from a Culture of Excellence

Journeys and roadmaps to excellence, such as the ANCC Magnet Recognition Program, describe the outcomes that attract and retain the most driven and caring nurses and deliver market-leading outcomes. As an Awakener, you contribute to reaching the following goals: mentoring and succession plans; high percentages of nurses certified in their specialty; increased numbers of nurses with a BSN degree; improved patient outcomes secondary to nurses' participation in professional development activities; effective transition to new roles; individualized professional development plans for nurses at all levels; commitment to a culture of safety; and improved results on nursing sensitive indicators (ANCC, 2015). These are not outcomes that can be initiated, accomplished, and checked off the list. Instead, these outcomes are produced and sustained as you give focused attention to maintaining the culture of excellence (Refer to Table 4).

Table 4

Crosswalk of ANCC (2015) Magnet Recognition Program Outcomes With Culture Change Influenced by the Human-Centered Leader Acting as an Awakener

Magnet Outcome Requirement	Human-Centered Leadership Dimension	Culture Change Required
Commitment to Culture of Safety	Awakener	Culture of Excellence
Mentoring plans	Awakener	Culture of Excellence
Decrease in never events / quality improvement based on EBP	Awakener	Culture of Excellence
Advancement of research in nursing / interprofessional	Connector/ Awakener	Culture of Trust/ Culture of Excellence

Increase percentage of nurses certified in their specialty.	Awakener	Culture of Excellence
Increase percentage of nurses with BSN degree.	Awakener	Culture of Excellence
Improve patient outcomes secondary to nurses' participation in professional development activities	Awakener	Culture of Excellence
Effective transition to new roles	Awakener	Culture of Excellence
Individualized professional development plans for nurses at all levels based on performance review, etc.	Awakener	Culture of Excellence

Note: From Leclerc, L., Kennedy, K., & Campis, S. (2021). Human-centered leadership in healthcare: A contemporary nursing leadership theory generated via constructivist grounded theory. *Journal of Nursing Management*, 29, 294–306.

Practical Ways to Influence a Culture of Excellence

Create Individual Development Plans

As an Awakener, ensure that each nurse has an individual development plan. This plan is initiated, developed, and owned by the staff member while you serve as a mentor, coach, and advocate to support the plan. A sample is provided in Table 5. Each goal is best described using the SMART format (specific, measurable, achievable, relevant, and time-based). Together with the nurse, determine the activities and resources required to accomplish the goal as well as the measure of success and target date for completion. The plan should include professional growth and educational goals as well as goals to support self-care and mindfulness to enhance resiliency and work/life balance. The plan may look different in each organization as it can be adapted from an existing ladder-type program, pillars of excellence, and organizational goals. It's important the plan is individualized to each team member, even if the format for the plan is standardized for the organization. For consistent follow-up, the plan should be reviewed and revised with every performance appraisal. Celebrate pertinent milestones and achievements with the team. Calling the team's attention to the growth and development of their colleagues through celebrations of milestones helps to sustain the culture of excellence.

Table 5

Sample Professional Development Plan

Long-Term Goals (3-5 years)					
SMART GOAL	**WHAT RESOURCES ARE NEEDED**	**WHO CAN HELP**	**REVIEW DATE**	**REVIEW DATE**	**ACHIEVED DATE**
Become a proficient, certified Surgical Trauma ICU Nurse in a Level I Trauma Center by 2024	Work in ICU for 2 years, progressively advancing in care of complex patients / Study for certification (online course) / Sit for Critical Care Registered Nurse (CCRN) specialty certification	ICU Manager / Charge RN / Peer Mentor			
Apply for MSN program at Emory University to begin in Sept 2025	Research of application process / Recommendation from previous managers	ICU Manager / 4S Manager			
Short-Term Goals (1-2 years)					
SMART GOAL	**WHAT RESOURCES ARE NEEDED**	**WHO CAN HELP**	**REVIEW DATE**	**REVIEW DATE**	**ACHIEVED DATE**
Personal Goals					
Practice Self-Care by improving sleep hygiene (in bed by 9:30 p.m. and up by 5:30 a.m.) beginning now (August 2021)	Discipline to turn off screens by 8:30 p.m. / Exercise on days off from work to help improve sleep.	Partner / Neighbor/ friend			
Begin using reflection to improve emotional intelligence and meet daily intentions beginning now (August 2021)	Reflection journal / Self-compassion when mistakes are made / Courage to make and keep daily intentions	Me			
Professional Goals					
Meet stated criteria and advance to Level 3 Staff nurse on Career Ladder by January 2022 performance review	Professional portfolio to provide evidence of meeting requirements / Opportunity to be a relief charge nurse / Opportunity to orient new staff and students	Manager / Peer Coach / Charge Nurse			
Become an active member on 4S unit NPG council by March 2022	Flexibility in schedule to attend meetings / Opportunity to lead an evidence-based quality improvement initiative on 4S	Manager / Peer Coach / NPG Chair			
Become a charge nurse on med-surg floor (preferably 4S) by August 2022	Begin *Human-Centered Leadership in Health Care* (HCL) virtual interactive program in January 2023 / Orient to charge nurse role beginning June 2023	Manager			

Celebrate Certified Nurses Day

This opportunity for recognition goes a long way in contributing to the motivation of team members. Certified Nurses Day occurs every March 19, the birthday of Dr. Margretta "Gretta" Madden Styles, RN, EdD, FAAN, one of the greatest leaders in the field of nursing certification (ANCC, n.d.). To celebrate Certified Nurses Day, consider the following:

1. Post framed copies of the team members' certifications on the walls of the unit and celebrate milestones as the percentage of certified nurses on the unit increases.
2. Celebrate with a breakfast or lunch to recognize all certified nurses and provide information on certification to those not yet certified.

Develop a Peer Coaching Program

Peer coaching has been used in teacher education (Lam et al., 2002), medical education (Sekerka & Chao, 2003) and nursing education (Broscious & Saunders, 2001) for years but is relatively new to staff development and the clinical practice of bedside nurses and advance practice providers (Waddell & Dunn, 2005). Peer coaching provides an opportunity for peers to practice newly learned skills and benefit from the nonhierarchical feedback of another learner. The intended benefits are quality improvement and risk reduction. According to Waddell and Dunn (2005), peer coaching should always be voluntary, and partners should be able to select each other. It should be used for the purpose of self-improvement and not as a part of an official performance review. In addition to the benefits of reflective practice and self-directed learning, peer coaching encourages true collegiality (Waddell & Dunn, 2005).

1. Consider incorporating peer coaching in nurse residency programs.
2. Consider using peer coaching in programs designed for role transition.
3. What other opportunities are there in your organization for peer coaching?

Implement Visual Management Boards to Follow Quality Outcomes

Lean management provides a process control tool that is helpful when a new change, typically around quality improvement, is implemented. This tool may be referred to as "visual management" or simply a "performance board." The purpose of the board is to visually communicate improvement results to staff and leadership. Short staff huddles around the board will provide insight on progress towards improved quality initiatives and support an environment of continuous learning and improvement (Silver et al., 2016) (Refer to Figure 6). These huddles also provide an opportunity for nurses to give voice to potential problems and solutions. This is actually an informal venue for shared governance. Keep in mind there are other change management strategies to assist with quality improvement. We'll go into more detail in Chapter 11.

1. Consider using a visual management board to follow a new initiative to improve outcomes associated with a nursing quality indicator, e.g. patient falls, pressure ulcers, central line associated blood stream infection (CLABSI), or catheter-associated urinary tract infection (CAUTI).
2. Enhance team collaboration through shared leadership of daily huddles around the board.

Recognize a Just Culture is a Safe Culture

Creating a *just culture* in an organization requires shifting the focus from judgement of errors and outcomes to focusing on their origins. The discussion revolves around system design and behavioral choices so that learning can occur, and good systems can support good caregivers. The expectation of perfection is taken off the table and the goal of safe practices is substituted. Just culture isn't punitive or blame-free. Instead, it supports professional accountability and results in a psychologically safer environment to practice and better outcomes for patients and families (Marx, 2019).

1. Recognize and celebrate those who report a near miss in unit or hospital safety huddles.
2. Refer near misses to NPG council for the development of innovative solutions for potential problems.

Figure 6

Performance board to monitor the home dialysis quality improvement project.

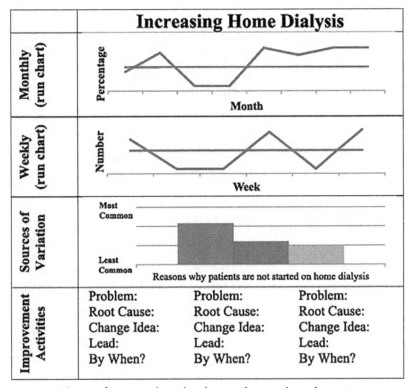

Note: This performance board indicates the team's goal—to increase the percentage of new patients started on home dialysis. Performance towards the goal is charted on a monthly and weekly basis. The causes of the variances are identified so that the team can propose change ideas to solve the root problems leading to variances From Silver, S. A., McQuillan, R., Harel, Z., Weizman, A. V., Thomas, A., Nesrallah, G., Bell, C. M., Chan, C. T., & Chertow, G. M. (2016). How to sustain change and support continuous quality improvement. *Clinical Journal of American Society of Nephrology*, 11(5), 916-24.

DISCUSSION QUESTIONS

1. What are the metrics you currently follow to ensure a culture of excellence?

2. What structure do you have in place to encourage staff participation in innovative problem-solving?

3. As a leader, develop SMART goals to improve your practice as the Awakener. Include goals and progress around the following: motivator, coach, mentor, architect, and advocate. Discuss your goals with your colleagues. How will you work together and harness the wisdom of the team? How can you help each other?
4. What do you need to move forward with creating and supporting professional development plans for your nurses?
5. How can you infuse the environment in your unit or department with the expectation of continuous growth and learning?
6. What resources do you have available to you to promote growth and learning among your staff? What else is needed?

REFLECTION

Think about your own professional growth and call to mind any leaders who acted as an Awakener by motivating, mentoring, and coaching you. How has this leader impacted your career and your life? Consider letting this leader know about their influence on your life. Recognizing people and thanking those who are important to you will contribute to your overall happiness and joy in life.

_____

_____

_____

_____

_____

_____

REFERENCES

American Nurses Credentialing Center. (2015). *ANCC Magnet Recognition Program.* https://www.nursingworld.org/organizational-programs/magnet/
American Nurses Credentialing Center. (n.d.). *ANCC Celebrate Certified Nurses.* https://www.nursingworld.org/education-events/certified-nurses-day/

American Organization of Nurse Executives (2015, April 15). *Future of nursing: Empowering leaders igniting change* [Video]. YouTube. https://www.youtube.com/watch?v=ytAV0jcIVPc

Broscious, S. K., & Saunders, D. J. (2001). Peer coaching. *Nurse Educator*, 26, 212–214.

Lam, S.-F., Yim, P.-S., & Lam, T. W.-H. (2002). Transforming school culture: Can true collaboration be initiated? *Educational Research*, 44, 181–195.

Leclerc, L., Kennedy, K., & Campis, S. (2020). Human-centered leadership in healthcare: An idea that's time has come. *Nursing Administration Quarterly*, 44(2), 117–126.

Leclerc, L., Kennedy, K., & Campis, S. (2021). Human-centered leadership in healthcare: A contemporary nursing leadership theory generated via constructivist grounded theory. *Journal of Nursing Management, 29*, 294–306.

Marx, D. (2019). Patient safety and just culture. *Obstetrics and Gynecology Clinics of North America.* 46(2), 239-245. https://doi.org/10.1016/j.ogc.2019.01.003

Porter-O'Grady, T., & Malloch, K. (2018). *Quantum Leadership: Creating Sustainable Value in Health Care* (5th ed.). Jones & Bartlett.

Sekerka, L. E., & Chao, J. (2003). Peer coaching as a technique to foster professional development in clinical ambulatory settings. *Journal of Continuing Education in the Health Professions*, 23, 30–37.

Silver, S. A., McQuillan, R., Harel, Z., Weizman, A. V., Thomas, A., Nesrallah, G., Bell, C. M., Chan, C. T., & Chertow, G. M. (2016). How to sustain change and support continuous quality improvement. *Clinical Journal of American Society of Nephrology*, 11(5), 916-24

Waddell, D. L., & Dunn, N. (2005). Peer coaching: The next step in staff development. *The Journal of Continuing Education in Nursing*, 36(2), 84–89.

Tye, J., & Dent, B. (2017). *Building a culture of ownership in healthcare*. Sigma Theta Tau International Honor Society of Nursing.

RECOMMENDED READING

O'Donovan, R., Ward, M., De Brun, A., & McAuliffe, E. (2019). Safety culture in health care teams: A narrative review of the literature. *Journal of Nursing Management*, 27(5), 871–883. https://doi.org/10.1111/jonm.12740.

Sherman, R. O. (2019). *The nurse leader coach: Become the boss no one wants to leave*. Rose O. Sherman.

Schwellnus, H., & Carnahan, H. (2014). Peer-coaching with health care professionals: What is the current status of the literature and what are the key components necessary in peer-coaching? *Medical Teacher*, 36(1), 38-46.

Studer, Q. (2003). *Hardwiring excellence*. Fire Starter Publishing.

Chapter 8

The Connector: Creating a Culture of Trust

"If you want to build a ship, don't summon people to buy wood, prepare tools, distribute jobs, and organize the work. Instead, teach people the yearning for the wide, boundless ocean."
—**Antoine de Saint-Exupéry**, "Citadelle"

The story below illustrates the Human-Centered Leader's impact in the complex system of healthcare. Specifically, you will see how demonstrating the attributes of the Connector leads to a healthy work environment and a culture of trust.

Exemplar

I had a unique experience as the CNO of a large community hospital, which taught me a great way to impact patient experience scores. It involved a solution that was initiated from *within* the organization rather than from the top. A middle manager in the pharmacy, Sabrina, was concerned about the fact that one question on the patient experience survey consistently received poor scores. It related to the patient's understanding of the side-effects of new medications. The exact question reads, "Before receiving new medications, how often did the hospital staff describe the medication side-effects in a way you could understand?" (U.S. Centers for Medicare and Medicaid Services, 2020). Sabrina thought there must be some way to improve this score, and she sincerely wanted the patients to be given information on their new medications. The problem seemed straightforward, especially since the nursing and pharmacy teams already had a strong working relationship. If it could be done, Sabrina thought the pharmacy and nursing teams could accomplish the improvement together.

Sabrina asked me for support and help in putting together a committee of interested nurse leaders and bedside caregivers. She was certain she could get her colleagues in the pharmacy involved. I was intrigued and excited about Sabrina's thoughts on collaborative problem-solving and went to work pulling together nurse leaders, nurse educators, and the patient experience team in preparation for the upcoming meeting. The nurse leaders were asked to bring any interested staff nurses along with them. The first meeting was designed to discuss the problem, consider barriers, and as time permitted, brainstorm possible solutions. In the first meeting, the team filled the boardroom, and I was witness to what Crowell (2016) describes as a "surprise" that emerged from the creativity of those intimately involved in self-organizing at the point of care.

One of the bedside nurses, a new graduate named Jermaine, attended the meeting. He had been a nurse less than one year, yet he was tech savvy and had previous experience working in graphic design and with teams. He spoke up, humbly offering a possible solution. Jermaine started by reviewing the problem as he saw it. He talked about issues such as health illiteracy, patients and staff members for whom English was their second or third language, and the ever-present concern in patient care of "information overload." There were also problems from the perspective of the nurses, such as time constraints and patients with numerous medications. Jermaine then pointed to a solution that he thought might address these barriers. He held up his laptop and began flipping through pages on his computer showing one screen after another of emojis representing different physical symptoms. One was green with nausea, another sported a big purple bruise, and still another had swirly, dizzy eyes. They all illustrated potential side effects of medications. His idea was to use the common language of emojis to communicate the side effects of medications to patients.

He thought this would provide the patients with a clear understanding and be efficient for the nurses as well. Jermaine suggested that the nurse give the patient some type of small card to display the name of the medication and the emoji illustrations of the side effects. The patient could take the card home at discharge as a reminder of this important information.

The team was elated! This was indeed a creative solution. Others on the team joined in to add their creative ideas. Over the next couple of months, a graphic artist was hired, cards were designed for the most often prescribed medications, a system for storing and distributing the cards was developed, and the workflow for the staff was established. This solution, which came from a staff member, was much more sensitive to the barriers experienced at the point of care than any solutions that could have been developed from leaders at the top of the organization.

Unfortunately, the scores did not respond immediately to the change. There were problems with the new workflow resulting in inconsistencies among caregivers. In addition, some medications didn't have an associated side-effects card because those meds weren't in the top tier of "most commonly prescribed medications." Despite the challenges, each discipline worked to fine-tune their part of the process and make this seemingly simple solution a part of the normal, but complex, workflow.

After a few months, solid and consistent improvement in the patient experience scores did follow, and the team was invited to present the project at the annual national meeting for Press Ganey, the industry's recognized leader in patient experience. This was a professional high for the team as they received many accolades for the success of their collaborative and innovative solution.

This story exemplifies the complexity of the healthcare organization, due to their interconnectedness and unpredictability. The team self-organized. The pharmacy, the nursing staff, and the patient experience team were all intricately connected, and this solution emerged from their collective wisdom. All I had to do was provide the environment for the solution to emerge, to be explored, and to be sustained. In a situation such as this, when the solution comes from within, there is no need for micromanaging, "holding the team accountable," or overreacting to inconsistencies in the data. The team makes it happen. As a result, they are accountable for the outcomes, and they are to be recognized for their creative solution.

Table 6

Defined Attributes Embodied by the Human-Centered Leader as a Connector

Connector	Builds our community
Collaborator	Unifies others around shared mission and vision
Supporter	Supports, recognizes, and appreciates independent problem-solving and individual contributions at the point of service
Edgewalker	Embraces change/chaos by endorsing experimentation with ideas to generate innovation
Engineer	Ensures people are plugged into processes/structures for emergence of new ideas
Authentic Communicator	Builds mutual respect and trust through nurturing intentional connections with others

Note: Adapted from Leclerc, L., Kennedy, K., & Campis, S. (2020). Human-centered leadership in healthcare: An idea that's time has come. *Nursing Administration Quarterly*, 44(2), 117-126 and Leclerc, L., Kennedy, K., & Campis, S. (2021). Human-centered leadership in healthcare: A contemporary nursing leadership theory generated via constructivist grounded theory. *Journal of Nursing Management*, 29, 294-306.

Who is the Connector?

The Human-Centered Leader, embedded in the work, turns their leadership focus outward to the staff by embodying the attributes of the Connector. The attributes include: collaborator, supporter, edgewalker, engineer, and authentic communicator (Refer to Table 6). By embracing these attributes, you, as the leader, demonstrate your belief in the team and their ability to unite around the mission, vision, and values of the organization. A quote from Stanley McChrystal (2015), retired general, author, and teams expert, sums up the leader's role as a Connector:

The temptation to lead as a chess master, controlling each move of the organization, must give way to an approach as a gardener, enabling rather than directing. A gardening approach to leadership is anything but passive. The leader acts as an "Eyes-On, Hands-Off" enabler who creates and maintains an ecosystem in which the organization operates. (p. 232)

As you learn more about the attributes of the Connector in the sections below, notice the direct quotes the nurses participating in our research used when describing their experiences with the leaders they valued most along their journey (Refer to Table 7).

Figure 7

The Connector

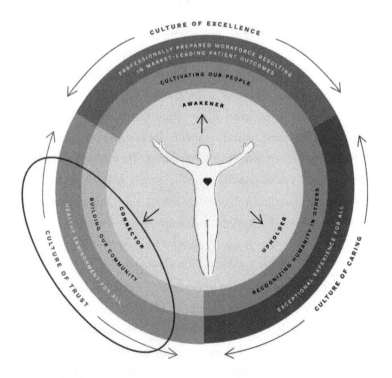

Note: Adapted from Leclerc, L., Kennedy, K., & Campis, S. (2020). Human-centered leadership in healthcare: An idea that's time has come. *Nursing Administration Quarterly*, *44*(2), 117-126.

Collaborator

When you think about collaborating, do you primarily consider working together with other leaders across the organization, or do you also consider working together with your team? Remember that Human-Centered Leaders position themselves within the team rather than above it. From your vantage point, at the center of the work, you'll be well positioned to listen to the team, understand their needs, remove barriers, and engage their creativity and capability to resolve problems. Your focus as a Connector is to unite them around the mission, vision, and values of the organization. Simply put, the Connector brings unity to the community! And the way you bring people together is through collaboration. The more diverse your team, the greater the potential impact they'll have as you leverage the strengths of each team member.

Nurse participants in our research stated that the leader they would "follow to the end of the earth" collaborates by "identifying the goal" and providing "support" to the team in their efforts. These leaders "show interest in the team members' work and abilities." The nurses called these leaders "opinion seekers" who understand the practice of appreciative inquiry and are eager to gather insight from different team members. These nurses noticed when leaders "actually listened" to their responses and opinions. They said these valued leaders also "offered choices" when possible and "honored and supported" the team's decisions. One nurse stated that the leader "respects the analytical nature of team members," which reflects the leader's understanding of the team's perspective.

Collaborator in Action: Josie, a nurse leader in critical care, was faced with a problem around patient flow. The busy ED in a large public hospital was not able to move patients to the ICU promptly. Even after the bed was assigned, giving report and transporting the critical patient was taking too long. Josie learned of a similar hospital that made progress on this issue by having the ICU nurse go to the ED for bedside handoff and then transport the patient to their ICU bed. The ICU staff was not in favor of this idea. Josie met with both teams together on a weekly basis, listened to their different perspectives, asked for their ideas, and supported their progress. Josie kept the focus on the common goal of improving the care from the patient's perspective. After a couple of months, the teams began to collaborate with each other. They developed a handoff tool and established a process to address problems in real time. Josie modeled collaboration for the team, and in time, they began to collaborate with each other. It took time to build trust, respect, and establish relationships. It required each team to understand the perspective of the other side. Josie was successful in her collaborative efforts, but more importantly, the patients were better served as a result of the unity between the teams and individuals.

Supporter

What does it mean to "support" your team and team members? Hopefully, you've had the experience of being supported by a leader and have felt empowered, secure, respected, and trusted as a result. These feelings of validation give us the freedom to perform at our best. A leader's genuine support abolishes our fear and allows us to learn from mistakes. We become free to stretch, to create and innovate. As you support your team and team members, your trust in their expertise and abilities will unleash their sense of empowerment. They may surprise you with their ability to creatively solve problems and contribute to a healthy work environment.

In our research, nurses described leaders who possessed traits of a Supporter with statements such as, "They openly demonstrate their confidence in the team and trust that the work will be done." They are "kind" to each individual and "understand that each person is fighting their own battles" (See Table 7).

Supporter in Action: The manager of an ICU, José, was concerned about the increase in CLABSIs among their critical patients. He met with the nurses on the unit and clearly shared with them his concerns around the trend in this data. He humbly stated that he did not have the answers, but he was confident in the team's ability to determine any gaps in care and develop a solution to this patient safety concern. He trusted their expertise and knowledge and was there to support their efforts. The team worked together in their NPG council, researched best practices, and developed innovative solutions. They sought out a superior central line dressing for their patient population. They also established a "buddy system" to use during sterile central line dressing changes to ensure compliance with the dressing change checklist. José's support allowed the team the freedom to explore possible solutions, which led to improved patient outcomes by decreasing the number of CLABSIs. In addition, José's support reinforced their confidence in their abilities to innovate and improve care.

Edgewalker

The term "edgewalker" was defined by Neal (2006) as someone who walks the precipice between two worlds with differing views and perspectives about organizational leadership. One world represents the traditional style of leadership and the other represents the contemporary, complexity style of leadership, like the Human-Centered Leadership approach. Alignment with both worlds is important to maintain the necessary tension between holding essential processes intact, while also being open to unpredictability and change. If there was no room for uncertainty, there would be no change and no movement towards innovative problem-solving.

The nurses participating in our research experienced edgewalkers as leaders who bring the team along with them. They have the "ability to get staff buy-in," and easily see and communicate the "big picture." They are comfortable being a "part of the process" rather than one who dictates the process. They are open to the surprise that an innovative person or team contributes, and they embrace creative solutions. They "appreciate people who think differently."

The Edgewalker in Action: Cindy, a nurse leader challenged with the goal of preparing bedside staff for the upcoming Joint Commission triannual visit, brought together a team of nurse educators and clinical nurse specialists to work together on this project. Cindy explained to the team that there was concern among the executive team that bedside nurses were not aware of new regulatory requirements. In the past, this would have required massive audits to determine nurses' gaps in knowledge, followed by education sessions, and then repeated audits. The team thought there must be a better way. Cindy was completely open and welcomed new, creative ideas. Through brainstorming and synergy, the team decided to develop a Joint Commission Information Fair. They identified the areas that nurses needed to learn about and came up with games to teach the new information. They set up a "fair" and developed a schedule that allowed every nurse to attend. The nurses played Jeopardy, Go Fish, and Password. They easily learned the new regulations, in a new way, and the Joint Commission survey was very successful! Cindy was an edgewalker who was willing to risk a new, creative approach to solving a problem that carried a high risk.

Engineer

As an engineer, the Connector looks at the big picture and plugs team members into the process in a way that identifies and values their strengths. Once you, as the leader, determine agreement on different roles within the team, your job, according to our research participants, is to "allow, support, and expect autonomy." As a result, your followers will act on their empowerment and do their jobs to meet the goal. The team is accountable for their results, and there is no need for micromanaging.

Engineer in Action: Think back to the story about Jermaine and the collaborative team who developed the cards with medication side effects illustrated through the common language of emojis. Each member on the team worked in the area of their strength. Pharmacists worked on the list of the most commonly prescribed medications and side-effects, nurse educators worked on establishing and teaching the workflow, and the patient experience team members worked with the graphic artist to bring the design to life. As this team evolved and the excitement grew, others wanted to be involved in the work. Executive assistants jumped in to work on the logistics of purchasing the storage boxes and ordering supplies. Each team member generously gave their time and expertise, worked autonomously in their area of strength, and the entire team succeeded as a result.

Authentic Communicator

We all know authentic communication when we see it, and ironically, you will best demonstrate authenticity through engaged listening. Active and engaged listening results in an interpersonal connection. The nurses in our research described this communication as "forthright," a "two-way conversation," "transparent," and "not political." As you harness your skills at "conflict resolution," others will see your intention of welcoming differences of opinion. Authentic communication will lead to a "safe" environment where team members feel free to express themselves. Be honest, demonstrate integrity, be trustworthy, and respect each person on the team. Be true to your word by doing what you say you will do. Lastly, honor the importance of confidentiality in your interactions to demonstrate your integrity and respect for the team, i.e., "don't gossip."

Authentic Communicator in Action: Every year, Lisa, the nurse manager of an ICU, knew her team would take the employee engagement survey and she would be required to develop an action plan around their responses. Even though Lisa had a good relationship with her team, she always worried a bit about what their comments would reveal. Did they think she was doing a good job? Were there problems on the unit she wasn't aware of? The time came and the survey results were in. Thankfully, most of the comments about the work environment were positive but there was a consistent negative comment about Lisa. Team members thought that she played favorites. Lisa was quite upset because she had no idea that she was giving this impression. She called a staff meeting to develop an action plan. As the meeting progressed, the discussion turned to Lisa and the issue of favoritism. Lisa listened carefully, and with empathy, to the staff. She was able to see the situation through their eyes, and she genuinely apologized for her lack of external self-awareness. She spoke from the heart about her intentions and her desire to engage completely with each of them in an equitable manner. She committed that she would do her best to change this perception and asked the team in return to commit to letting her know if they noticed a problem. Lisa's authentic communication proved to be an opportunity for further trust and connection between her and the team.

Table 7

Qualitative Research Connecting Participant Feedback
with Concepts and Attributes of the Connector

Connector: Building our Community → Culture of Trust		
Category/Concept	**Participant Comments and In Vivo Codes**	**Attribute**
Communication	a. "Forthright" b. "Two-way conversation" c. "Transparent, not political" d. Good at conflict resolution e. Safe environment f. "Don't be a 'yes' man…let me in on the 'why' if it can't be supported" g. Will disagree with you	Authentic Communicator
Empowering	a. Autonomy: "allows it, supports it, expects it" b. Confidence in team: "appreciates that work will get done" c. Supported: helps identify and resolve barriers d. "Identify the goal, then support me…offers some autonomy…shows interest in my work and abilities" e. "Opinion seeker" seeks my opinion f. "Seeks opinions and actually listens" g. Offers choices and honors and supports them h. "Respects analytical nature of team members"	Engineer Supporter Collaborator

Trustworthy	a. Integrity, Honesty (mentioned multiple times) b. Leader's trust is earned c. "Respect is earned" d. Does not gossip, is not "catty" e. Offers "safe space" and encourages a culture of honesty f. Kind to everyone and understands that staff are human and are fighting life's battles g. Gives credit where credit is due	Authentic Communicator Supporter
Innovative	a. Ability to get staff "buy in" b. Ability to see the big picture c. Be a part of the process d. Understand and embrace change versus "we have always done it this way" e. Attitude that "we may lose the battle, but we will win the war" f. "Appreciates people who think differently	Edgewalker

Note: From Leclerc, L., Kennedy, K., & Campis, S. (2021). Human-centered leadership in healthcare: A contemporary nursing leadership theory generated via constructivist grounded theory. *Journal of Nursing Management*, 29, 294–306.

The Connector Meets Complexity

The attributes of the Connector clearly link the Human-Centered Leader to the foundations of complexity science and complex adaptive systems (CAS). Remember Jermaine and his team who developed the emoji cards to influence patient outcomes and satisfaction? Jermaine's story illustrates that connected work groups, united in their pursuit of the organization's mission and vision, can create innovative solutions. How does that happen? Is it predictable? Stacy (1996) and Eoyang (1997) outline the parameters of complex adaptive systems, which are clearly recognizable in our story: information flows freely; there is a rich connectivity; there are diverse mental models; there is diversified leadership; and there are simple rules. The team was given free rein to create a solution to the problem around patients' understanding of the side-effects of their new medications. The members shared their different perspectives and connected processes. The rules were simple—no constraints were put in place. The leadership was diversified as team members gravitated toward their individual areas of strength. The stage was set for self-organization and innovation. Creative ideas, like the one Jermaine shared, emerge from within a complex system and can have a huge impact on the organization. The proposed solution by a new nurse graduate produced what is known in complexity science as the "butterfly effect." His small contributions resulted in big outcomes for the organization.

Outcomes Resulting from a Culture of Trust

According to The Great Places to Work model, the values of credibility, respect, and fairness create **trust**. When you act as a Connector, you demonstrate these values through authentic communication, support, collaboration, plugging people into the appropriate structures for collaborative problem-solving (engineer), and extending trust to the team by encouraging innovation around change and unpredictability (edgewalker). The American Association of Critical Care Nurses (AACN) describes this type of trusting culture as a "healthy work environment." There is an extensive body of nursing research on the criteria for developing healthy work environments and the associated positive outcomes for nurses and patients. To put it simply, nurses who work in trusting environments are more fulfilled in their work, and their patients receive safe and high-quality care.

As you practice the attributes of the Connector, your leadership skills will contribute to a culture of trust and your outcomes will align closely with those required by the ANCC Magnet Recognition Program standards (2015). The ANCC Magnet Recognition Program requires *sustained* quality outcomes that are attributable to a positive, healthy culture. We've all heard Peter Drucker's famous quote, "Culture eats strategy for breakfast." Positive outcomes result from a positive culture rather than from new initiatives. The ANCC standards require organizations to: improve the nurses' practice environments; to connect with the community through an outward focus on health populations; to deliver care that is culturally and socially sensitive; to establish nurse to nurse and interprofessional collaboration; and to work collaboratively on the advancement of research to continually improve practice (Refer to Table 8). Achieving these results is the work of a Human-Centered Leader who understands and practices the attributes of the Connector.

Table 8

Crosswalk of ANCC (2015) Magnet Recognition Program Outcomes with Culture Change Influenced by the Human-Centered Leader Acting as a Connector

Magnet Outcome Requirement	Human-Centered Leadership Dimension	Culture Change Required
Improved nursing practice environment	Connector	Culture of Trust
Nurse involvement in population heath outreach	Connector	Culture of Trust
Delivery of culturally and socially sensitive care	Connector	Culture of Trust
Nurses and interprofessional groups contribute to strategic goals of organization	Connector	Culture of Trust
Advancement of research in nursing/interprofessional	Connector/ Awakener	Culture of Trust/ Culture of Excellence

Note: From Leclerc, L., Kennedy, K., & Campis, S. (2021). Human-centered leadership in healthcare: A contemporary nursing leadership theory generated via constructivist grounded theory. *Journal of Nursing Management, 29,* 294–306.

Practical Ways to Influence a Culture of Trust

Embrace AACN's Standards for a Healthy Work Environment

AACN provides standards required for a healthy work environment: Authentic communication, true collaboration, effective decision-making, appropriate staffing, meaningful recognition, and authentic leadership.

1. Ask your team to take the AACN Healthy Work Environment assessment, which you can find on the AACN website, to determine strengths and areas for improvement.

2. Ask team members to work through NPG on specific strategies to improve the work environment.

3. Embrace Vital Smarts *Silence Kills,* an industry study, and support the team in practicing crucial conversations (Maxfield et.al., 2005).

4. Recognize the strengths individual team members possess and plug them into the NPG and other committee opportunities where their strengths will be best used.

5. Work with your team to determine how to best reward and recognize those who are excelling and contributing to the mission, vision, and values of the unit and organization.

6. Establish a zero-tolerance policy for incivility and bullying.

7. Make respect for each other a palpable value in the workplace.

8. Engage team members in developing creative staffing models to meet the needs of patients and leverage staff working collaboratively and at "top of license."

9. Trust your team and the decisions made through the NPG.

10. What other ways can you support the development of a healthy workenvironment? —————————————————————

—————————————————————

—————————————————————

DISCUSSION QUESTIONS

1. Which staff members are involved in your NPG councils? Are your teams diverse and inclusive? Are people plugged into the areas where their strengths shine?

2. Is your team involved in any research around improving clinical practice? How can you support this process?

3. How has your team collaborated across the system? Is there a structure in place to ensure this communication and collaboration occurs?

4. Does your team see you as an edgewalker? How do you demonstrate to the team that you are open to change and innovation? How do you embrace unpredictability?

REFLECTION

Have your team take the AACN *Healthy Work Environment* assessment provided on the AACN website. What are the strengths of your current environment? What areas need your attention? What will you do to make the needed improvements?

_____

_____

_____

_____

_____

REFERENCES

American Nurses Credentialing Center. (2015). *ANCC Magnet Recognition Program.* https://www.nursingworld.org/organizational-programs/magnet/

American Association of Critical Care Nurses. (n.d.). *AACN Standards for establishing and sustaining healthy work environments: A journey to excellence* (2nd ed.). https://www.aacn.org/~/media/aacn-website/nursing-excellence/healthy-work-environment/execsum.pdf?la=enhttps://www.aacn.org/membership/signin?ReturnUrl=http://mini.aacn.org/dm/HWE/TabbedAdminHome.aspx

Centers for Medicare and Medicaid Service. (n.d.). Retrieved October 8, 2020 from https://hcahpsonline.org/en/survey-instruments/

Crowell, D. M. (2016). *Complexity Leadership* (2nd ed.). FA Davis Co.

Eoyang, G.H. (1997). Coping with chaos: Seven simple tools. Lagumo.

Great Place to Work. (n.d.). *The definition of a great workplace.* Retrieved October 17, 2020 from www.greatplacetowork.com/trust

Leclerc, L., Kennedy, K., & Campis, S. (2020). Human-centered leadership in healthcare: An idea that's time has come. *Nursing Administration Quarterly,* 44(2), 117–126.

Leclerc, L., Kennedy, K., & Campis, S. (2021). Human-centered leadership in healthcare: A contemporary nursing leadership theory generated via constructivist grounded theory. *Journal of Nursing Management, 29,* 294–306.

Maxfield, D., Grenny, J., McMillan, R., Patterson, K., & Switzler, A. (2005). *Silence kills: The seven crucial conversations for healthcare.* Vital Smarts Industry Watch. https://www.aacn.org/nursing-excellence/healthy-work-environments/~/media/aacn-website/nursing-excellence/healthy-work-environment/silencekills.pdf?la=en

McChrystal, S., Collins, T., Silverman, D., & Fussell, C. (2015). *Team of teams: New rules of engagement for a complex world.* Penguin.

Neal, J. (2006). *Edgewalkers: People and organizations that take risks, build bridges, and break new ground.* Praeger.

Stacey, R. D. (1996). *Complexity and creativity in organizations.* Berrett-Koehler.

RECOMMENDED READING

Patterson, K., Grenny, J., McMillan, J. & Switzler, A. (2004). *Crucial confrontations: Tools for resolving broken promises, violated expectations, and bad behavior.* McGraw Hill.

Patterson, K., Grenny, J., McMillan, R., Switzler, A. (2008). *Influencer: The power to change anything.* McGraw Hill.

Patterson, K., Grenny, J., McMillan, R., Switzler, A. (2012). *Crucial conversations: Tools for talking when stakes are high* (2nd ed.). McGraw Hill.

Thompson, R. (2013). *"Do no harm" applies to nurses too!* Incredible Messages Press.

Thompson, R. (2019). Enough! Eradicate bullying and incivility in healthcare. Incredible Messages Press.

Chapter 9

The Upholder: Cultivating a Culture of Caring

"Leadership is not about being in charge. Leadership is about taking care of those in your charge."

—**Simon Sinek**, British-American Author,
Leadership Expert, and Inspirational Speaker

There are some leaders who know how to *effectively* care for their team members—not like a "mama," who is overly protective and micromanages them—but more like a compassionate colleague or friend. This type of leader is focused on well-being for both themselves and others, and on inspiring individuals to embrace all they are and all they can become. Through the story below, I hope you develop a better understanding of the attributes of the Upholder and your ability to positively impact the members of your team.

Exemplar

Evalyn, an executive nurse director over a large service line, embodied the practice of transformational interactions through intentional listening and empathetic understanding of her staff (Porter-O'Grady & Malloch, 2018).

Through intent listening, empathy, and acceptance, she gained the staff's respect and more importantly, she changed the way the staff viewed themselves. Evalyn's official position was in executive leadership, yet she embraced the opportunity to embed herself within the team. It was through her approach as an Upholder that she was able to transform a previously poorly engaged unit into the highest functioning unit in the organization. Don't get me wrong, it wasn't a quick, instant fix. In fact, it took a couple of years, but the outcomes that resulted from the culture of caring Evalyn developed have been sustained long after she moved on to another position.

When Evalyn joined the leadership team, she encountered an uphill battle. The staff were not at all receptive to her. They feared that she wouldn't "advocate" for them, that she was "on the side of management," and that she had never "walked in their shoes" and couldn't understand their perspective. Evalyn had not risen from the ranks of the organization. She was from the "outside" and this, in and of itself, created a sense of uncertainty among the team. They didn't know what changes she might put in place and, more importantly, how those changes might impact them. Even as Evalyn was keenly aware of the team's attitude toward her, she stayed focused on her intention to strengthen the team by first embracing them and creating a culture where the team members authentically cared for each other and for their patients. Looking back, I realize that it was her emotional intelligence that allowed her to stay calm rather than become defensive, remain self-assured and self-confident in her leadership methods, and continually reach out to establish and manage relationships. One crucial key to her success was that she *always* gave the team credit for accomplishments, which reinforced her support and confidence in them and, in time, helped them to trust her.

Evalyn went about leading this team in a mindful, calm, and poised manner. She wore scrubs and worked alongside the staff whenever possible. She got to know the staff members as individuals. After a while, the staff realized that her engagement with them involved her full attention on their humanness, their strengths, and their good intentions. Evalyn is not one to blame or shame. Instead, she pulled the team together around their mission—patient safety and excellent patient care.

At the same time, Evalyn was no pushover. She held a high bar for engagement and service excellence and had to make the tough decisions to terminate a few staff members who were not willing to fully engage in the work. Some staff members self-selected out once they realized that the expectations had changed and, for whatever reason, they were not willing or able to make a change themselves. Evalyn held a high bar for engagement, service, and civility, and by doing so, she further endorsed the standards on the unit and created a culture of caring. She lived by the rule that leaders must hold high moral standards and follow ethical guidelines when addressing any disrespectful or disruptive behavior. At the same time, Evalyn ensured that staff were validated and rewarded for exemplary commitment to the values of the organization (Faith, 2014). By consistently modeling the organization's values and recognizing others for demonstrating those same values, Evalyn's leadership led to a culture of caring.

How did she do it? Evalyn is one of those people who is naturally curious about other people. She wants to know what motivates them, how they relate to the world, and what their values are. She demonstrated her values by being present, in mind and body, which allowed her to establish open, trusting relationships. She consistently rounded on all the staff and the patients, listening to their concerns, and responding with empathy and compassion. The staff recognized that it wasn't just the patients who mattered, nor was it just the metrics—it was them, the team. She was authentic in her actions. She could be counted on to mean and do what she said she would and to extend authentic caring to each staff member, patient, and family. Her actions demonstrated what Goldman (2013) described as "gifted leadership"—where the heart and the head meet.

As a result of Evalyn's leadership, the team became more engaged with each other, with their colleagues from other disciplines, and with their patients. Their engagement score moved up a tier on an organization-wide survey, and their patient experience scores topped out at the 99th percentile. The turnover rate decreased, and the unit was known to be a place where nurses wanted to work. Whenever an administrator, physician, nurse, or VIP was admitted to the hospital, they were admitted to this unit. Why? Because the unit's reputation was that patients received excellent care and the nursing staff was outstanding. These outcomes came about from a culture change—from the leadership behaviors attributed to the qualities of the Upholder, not from a newly established organization-wide initiative.

Table 9

Defined Attributes Embodied by the Human-Centered Leader as an Upholder

Upholder	Recognizes humanity in others
Mindful	Focuses attention, awareness, and energy on present
Others-Oriented	Supports with respect, kindness, empathy, and empowerment
Emotionally Aware	Recognizes and embraces humanity at all levels, self-reflective
Socially and Organizationally Aware	Leads with an open mind
Personally Well and Healthy	Practices self-care, self-compassion, self-awareness

Note: From Leclerc, L., Kennedy, K., & Campis, S. (2020). Human-centered leadership in healthcare: An idea that's time has come. *Nursing Administration Quarterly*, 44(2), 117-126 and Leclerc, L., Kennedy, K., & Campis, S. (2021). Human-centered leadership in healthcare: A contemporary nursing leadership theory generated via constructivist grounded theory. *Journal of Nursing Management*, 29, 294-306.

Who is the Upholder?

Our research with nurses revealed the following attributes were included within the Upholder's way of being: mindful, others-oriented, emotionally aware, socially and organizationally aware, and personally well and healthy (see Table 9). The nurses in our research study spoke specifically about leaders who understood work-life balance and took care of themselves (see Table 10). They said the leader modeled self-care to the team and encouraged them to establish a work-life balance as well.

Figure 8

The Upholder

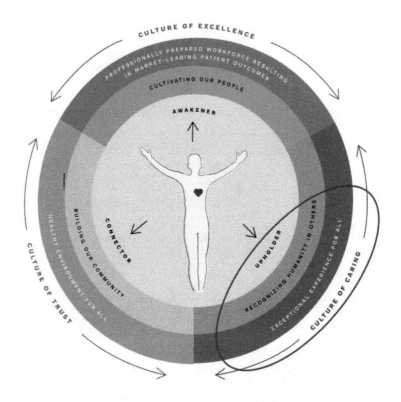

Note: Adapted from Leclerc, L., Kennedy, K., & Campis, S. (2020). Human-centered leadership in healthcare: An idea that's time has come. *Nursing Administration Quarterly, 44*(2), 117-126.

Mindful

The nurses participating in our research discussed the importance of mindfulness, which they recognized through the "openness" and "presence" required to "listen" and respond with "empathy" and "understanding." The nurses talked about leaders who "treated them like a person" and "related to their experiences." Williams et al. (2012) argue that the practice of mindfulness allows a person to let go of bias, preconceptions, judgements, and expectations of others. The leader as an Upholder is mindful of bias, highly values diversity and inclusivity within the team, and leaves judgement and negative assumptions behind (Leclerc et al. 2020).

Emotionally Aware

In addition, the nurses participating in our research talked about the emotional intelligence required of leaders. Emotional intelligence helps leaders "build relationships," "be respectful," and "appreciate humanity in others." It is emotional intelligence that allows the leader to recognize and understand emotions in themselves and others and to use this awareness to manage behaviors and relationships (Bradberry & Greaves, 2009). For more information on emotional intelligence refer to Chapter 10.

Others-Oriented

The nurses in our research study talked about leaders who were others-oriented. They identified an outward focus that could be described as "empathy," "advocacy," "supportiveness," and "compassion." One nurse said that the "leader reflected the staff, rather than the staff reflecting the leader." This likely means that each staff member felt highly valued and understood by the leader because they experienced others-oriented approach to leadership.

When you think about the term "others-oriented," does it bring to mind the value of compassion? Do you think about a leader's positive intentions and real concern for the well-being of others? While this is a correct description of compassion, understand that compassion alone is not enough. For effective leadership, compassion must be combined with wisdom. *Wise compassion* is the ability to do hard things in a human way. It means you can make hard decisions, give tough feedback, and when necessary, even lay off members of your team. Wise compassion means you balance concern for others **with** the need to move the organization forward in an effective manner (Hougaard et. al., 2020). If you've ever had to lay someone off and they responded positively with a "thank you," and maybe even a hug, you've probably got the right balance. If not, read on…

If you need more compassion to get the right balance, remember to embrace the other attributes of the Upholder—practice mindfulness and become intentionally aware of others' emotions. Start with yourself and practice self-compassion. Check your intentions before you have a direct and difficult conversation. Set your intention on providing a benefit to others. Lastly, practice compassion daily so it will become a habit for you (Hougaard et. al., 2020).

On the other hand, if your tendency is to weigh in heavier on the side of compassion, practice candid transparency. Remember your intention is to benefit others. Concealing criticism is misleading. Brené Brown (2018) is known for saying, "Being clear is kind. Being unclear is unkind." Try to practice having a direct and assertive interaction every day so you can make *wise compassion* a habit (Hougaard et. al., 2020).

The Mindful, Emotionally Aware, and Others-Oriented Leader in Action:

Jean Watson (2009), theorist and expert in the "Art of Caring," suggests the following ways to demonstrate **"Caring in Action,"** which correlate with these attributes of the Upholder:

- Creating intentional and meaningful rituals. For example, hand washing is for infection control, but also may be a meaningful ritual of self-care and mindfulness.
- Creating healing spaces for nurses: sanctuaries for their time out. May include meditation or relaxation rooms for quiet time.
- Intentionally pausing and breathing. For example, preparing self to be present before entering patients' rooms.
- Selecting caring-healing modalities for self and patients, e.g. massage, therapeutic touch, reflexology, aromatherapy, sound, music, arts, and a variety of energetic modalities.
- Dimming the unit lights and having designated "quiet time" for patients, families, and staff, to soften, slow down, and calm the environment.
- Engaging in caring rounds at patients' bedsides. For example, focus on non-physical aspects of care such as spiritual and emotional needs.

- Engaging in centering exercises and mindfulness practices as a group. For example, add a mindful moment to huddles.

(Watson, 2009)

Socially and Organizationally Aware

The quotes from nurses in our research study, in all positions of leadership, revealed the importance of self-awareness demonstrated through humility and the ability to recognize humanity in self and others. One nurse in the research study mentioned that a leader is "not always popular," but is self-assured and confident. The Upholder demonstrates self-management as they "adjust" and "support the team in stressful situations." The leader as Upholder is socially and organizationally aware, being careful not to "play favorites" but instead "give everyone a fair chance." When an Upholder is embedded within the team, the vision, work, and outcomes belong to the team rather than to the leader alone. Being socially and organizationally aware as an embedded leader is a hallmark of the Upholder. The Upholder is a liaison between potential competing priorities of upper leadership and the point-of-service priorities.

The Socially and Organizationally Aware Leader in Action:

Jean Watson, theorist and expert in the "Art of Caring" suggests the following ways to demonstrate **"Caring in Action,"** which correlate with these attributes of the Upholder:

- Creating healing environments—attending to the subtle environment. For example, paying attention to details in the environment such as uncluttered and organized nurse's station or patient rooms.
- Interviewing and selecting staff on basis of "caring" orientation. For example, asking candidates to describe a "Caring Moment."

- Making human caring integral to the organizational vision and culture. For example, integrate caring language into the vision, mission, and values statements.
- Placing reminders of caring practices in the environment. For example, place magnets on patient's door with positive affirmations.
- Exploring integration of caring language in documentation. For example, document "caring rounds."
- Displaying healing objects in accordance with patients' wishes, for example, prayer mats, crosses, stones, mandalas, and artwork.

(Watson, 2009)

Personally Well and Healthy

As you embody the traits of the Upholder, you will focus on personal resiliency and well-being, which is achieved through the practices discussed earlier: self-awareness, self-compassion, self-care, and mindfulness. Through modeling these "self" practices along with mindfulness, you will be better able to connect, care, and intentionally focus on others. In turn, the caregivers will appreciate the caring interactions and be influenced to assess and improve their own resiliency and wellness practices. As you model these practices, the team will realize the importance of prioritizing these habits in their own lives. Upholders can function as "point attractors," which Crowell (2016) describes as a pattern of behavior that attracts like behavior in a complex system. Through role-modeling wellness practices and demonstrating new ways of leading, the Upholder creates their own butterfly effect, meaning their seemingly small behaviors can have an enormous impact due to the sensitivity and interconnectivity of the staff and the structures within the organization.

Because of the nature of healthcare, the work environment on a unit needs to reflect care and caring. The team members want to feel comfortable, safe, cared for, and they want to know that they hold an important position within the organization. They want to feel that the work they're doing connects them to their purpose. While this can sound overwhelming for a leader, it's something that evolves as the culture changes, and over time a culture of caring develops. Nurses, as humans caring for other humans, must first show care for themselves and be cared for before they can do the same for others. We've all heard the phrase, "you can't give what you don't have." This simple wisdom explains why the work of the Human-Centered Leader, acting as an Upholder, is so important. Care for the caregivers results in an improved experience for all.

As an Upholder, you embrace your own humanity and demonstrate self-compassion when mistakes are made. You'll want to be whole-hearted and according to Brown (2010), that means inherently vulnerable. You are willing to take ownership of your mistakes and absorb criticisms. This is not the part of leadership that leaders enjoy thinking about. It does, however, reveal why leaders must be courageous to be authentic. The vulnerability and authenticity of a leader demonstrate strength rather than weakness and open the door for a strong connection and relationship with staff members.

The Personally Well and Healthy Leader in Action:
Watson (2009), theorist and expert in the "Art of Caring" suggests the following ways to demonstrate "**Caring in Action**," which correlate with these attributes of the Upholder:

- Cultivating your own spiritual practices.
- Cultivating heart-centered practices of loving kindness.
- Cultivating self-control and calm in yourself and others.
- Engaging in centering exercises.
- Engaging in mindfulness practices.
- Participating in multi-site research assessing caring among staff and patients.
- Creating opportunities to share caring moments.
- Creating innovative practice models or patterns around the delivery of care.

- Developing "caring competencies" to guide caring practice. For example, using active listening with patients and colleagues, sitting at the bedside when possible, and including family in the conversation.

Table 10

Qualitative Research Connecting Participant Feedback with Concepts and Attributes of the Attributes of the Upholder

Upholder: Recognizing Humanity in Others → Culture of Caring		
Category/ Concept	**Participant Comments and In Vivo Codes**	**Attribute**
Recognizes Humanity Humility	a. "Treats me like a person" b. Authentic (multiple) c. "School doesn't 'prepare' you for leadership, are leaders born?" d. Can build relationships e. Respectful as a person and position f. "Recognizes me as a unique individual" g. Compassionate h. "Has compassion for human aspect such as life health" i. Respects the leadership role j. Has ability to seek assistance when needed k. The leader reflects the team, who they are, not a reflection of the leader l. Selfless	Others Oriented Emotionally Aware
Self-Care	a. Role model for work/life balance b. Supports team members work/life balance c. "Work is only one part of life" d. "Having a leader who recognizes our team is better off if team members are 'healthy' with home and balance of work/life." e. "We're a caring profession…we need to learn to care for ourselves."	Personal Wellbeing

Fair	a. Doesn't play favorites b. Supports just culture c. Provides a safe environment d. Gives a "fair chance" to everyone. Example: If there is a patient complaint, a good leader will not only talk to the patient but will follow up with the nurse to hear her story. Not quick to "judge" e. Understands both sides f. Advocates for the nurse g. Respectful of everyone: "My manager is over two units, but she has the same expectations for each unit, she has no favorites and is consistent in her communication." h. "You work hard for me; I'll work hard for you." i. Fair with feedback, both good and bad j. "A fair leader is like a balance beam" k. Takes ownership of managers responsibilities l. "Not necessarily popular"	Socially and Organizationally Aware
Motherly	a. "Mama bear" b. Supportive c. Empathetic d. Defends staff e, Staff advocate	Others Oriented
Kind	a. Understanding b. Relates to staff experiences c. Always remembers "where she/he came from" d. Empathetic e. Present f. Has ownership of the team g. Listens	Mindful

| **Resilient** | a. Ability to bounce back
b. When responsibilities change, the leader does not complain or get frustrated. They adjust and continue to cheer on the team
c. "A unit with many new nurses experienced a Code Blue. This was the first code situation for many of the new nurses. The leader had the ability to support the nurses and continue with the code even though it was a stressful."
d. Offers support both physical and emotional."
e. Emotional intelligence | Socially and Organizationally Aware
Mindful |

Note: From Leclerc, L., Kennedy, K., & Campis, S. (2021). Human-centered leadership in healthcare: A contemporary nursing leadership theory generated via constructivist grounded theory. *Journal of Nursing Management*, 29, 294–306.

The Upholder Meets Complexity

As a leader embodying the Upholder attributes, you'll want to embrace the practice of self-reflection and be personally aware of your emotions. Through the intentional practice of mindfulness, your team will see that you are fully present in interactions with them, with colleagues, and with patients. Because Human-Centered Leadership is grounded in relationships, the Upholder attributes provide the foundation for authentic communication, openness, and the free flow of information. In a complex adaptive system, your commitment to nonhierarchical communication flow will lead to and foster interconnections. These interconnections among the team and across other disciplines lead to self-organization, which is where innovation originates. According to Crowell (2016), the quality of the team's relationships influences the quality of the healthcare outcomes.

The Upholder, who ensures that relationships are authentic, collaborative, and free from judgement, is the cornerstone on which self-organization, innovation, and positive outcomes develop.

Outcomes Resulting from a Culture of Caring

As we discussed earlier, when you as the leader focus on self-care, mindfulness, and well-being, you can impact the staff's prioritization of the same behaviors. Furthermore, a study by Barsade and O'Neill (2014) found that a culture of compassion at work contributes to decreased absenteeism and emotional exhaustion. Furunes et.al. (2018) also found that leaders who embrace self-care and personal wellness for themselves improves nurse retention. Other outcomes associated with a culture of caring include employee satisfaction, teamwork, patient mood, and patient satisfaction (Barsade & O'Neill, 2014).

The culture of caring goes beyond impacting the team and patients on a personal level. It also impacts quality care and safe practice by fostering team behaviors and collaboration. When mistakes happen, team members are more comfortable speaking up, knowing that they will not be blamed or shamed but instead that the team will support them and work to improve systems that will prevent the same mistake in the future. According to Watson (2007, 2009), a caring and supportive environment leads to a decrease in adverse events.

The ANCC Magnet Recognition Program requires empirical outcomes related to a culture of caring (Refer to Table 11). These outcomes include: decreased turnover rates, improved patient experience, greater responsiveness to patients' feedback (service recovery), and greater RN satisfaction, which includes access to leadership, the responsiveness of leaders, autonomy, interprofessional relationships, quality care, and adequate resources (ANCC, 2015).

Table 11

Crosswalk of ANCC (2015) Magnet Recognition Program Outcomes with Culture Change Influenced by the Human-Centered Leader acting as an Upholder

Magnet Outcome Requirement	Human-Centered Leadership Dimension	Culture Change Required
Decrease in turnover rate	Upholder	Culture of Caring
Improved patient experience	Upholder	Culture of Caring
Improvements based on patient feedback and service recovery	Upholder	Culture of Caring

RN satisfaction: leadership access and responsiveness	Upholder	Culture of Caring
RN satisfaction: autonomy; interprofessional relationships; fundamentals of quality; adequacy of resources and staffing	Upholder	Culture of Caring

Note: From Leclerc, L., Kennedy, K., & Campis, S. (2021). Human-centered leadership in healthcare: A contemporary nursing leadership theory generated via constructivist grounded theory. *Journal of Nursing Management*, 29, 294–306.

Practical Ways to Influence a Culture of Caring

Rounding

Latest best practices encourage managers to round on staff routinely. This practice helps connect the staff member to the leader and helps to build trust, rapport, and demonstrate caring. Watson's (2009) theory reinforces the need for leaders to ensure that staff feel cared for, have the resources they need, and have the support of a collaborative team. To create a culture of caring, ask the staff member during leader-staff rounds:

1. Do you feel cared for on this unit?
2. What would make you feel more cared for?
3. Do you have the tools and equipment you need to care for your patients?
4. Do you have the support of the team to provide the best care to your patients?

Recognizing Supportive Team Members

You will find that there are many ways to recognize your supportive team members. You'll need to determine which works best on your unit.

1. If you huddle during or at the end of the shift, ask if anyone can give a call-out to a team member for supporting them in caring for a patient.
2. Keep notes at a bulletin board and encourage staff to write a short note about a team member who supported them during the shift and post to the "TEAM" board.

3. What other ideas do you have?_____

_____

Make Self-Care and Work-Life Harmony a Priority for Yourself and Your Team Members

1. Ask team members what they are doing to take care of themselves. Make sure that the team is taking their lunch and dinner breaks, practicing mindful moments, using deep breathing for relaxing during breaks, and taking appropriate time off.

2. Encourage staff participation in wellness activities. One organization did a wellness challenge to see who could clock the most steps on their device over a period of one month. That winner was celebrated and received a membership at the organization's wellness center.

3. One CNO colleague does her one-on-one meeting with her directors as "walking" meetings as a way to promote wellness in self and others.

4. What other ideas do you have to prioritize well-being with you team?

_____

_____

DISCUSSION QUESTIONS

1. What are the metrics you currently follow to ensure a culture of caring?

2. What additional metrics could you consider to facilitate an environment where staff are satisfied and experience meaningful work and patients report positive experiences (Refer to Table 11)?

3. As a leader, develop SMART goals to improve your practice of the Upholder attributes. Include goals around the following: personal wellness, self-awareness, mindfulness, others-oriented mindset, and social and organizational awareness. Discuss your goals with your colleagues. How will you work together and harness the wisdom of the team? How can you help each other?

4. How can you infuse the environment with the expectation of positive staff interrelationships and caring service to your patients?

5. What resources do you have available to you to promote wellness, mindfulness, and positive relationships among your staff? What else is needed?

REFLECTION

Have you ever experienced a Culture of Caring? If this is your current experience, how will you continue to nurture and protect this culture? If this is not your current experience, how can you begin to impact the culture through care for yourself, your staff, and your patients?

_____

_____

_____

_____

_____

_____

REFERENCES

American Nurses Credentialing Center. (2015). ANCC Magnet Recognition Program. https://www.nursingworld.org/organizational-programs/magnet/>>

Barsade S. G., & O'Neill O. A. (2014). What's love got to do with it? A longitudinal study of the culture of companionate love and employee and client outcomes in a long-term care setting. *Administrative Science Quarterly*, 59, 551–98.

Bradberry, T., & Greaves, J. (2009). *Emotional intelligence 2.0.* TalentSmart.

Brown, B. (2010). *The gifts of imperfection: Let go of who you think you're supposed to be and embrace who you are.* Hazelden.

Brown, B. (2018, October 15). *Clear is kind. Unclear is unkind.* https://brenebrown.com/blog/2018/10/15/clear-is-kind-unclear-is-unkind/

Crowell, D. M. (2016). *Complexity Leadership* (2nd ed.). FA Davis Co.

Faith, K. (2013). The role of value-based leadership in sustaining a culture of caring. *Healthcare Management Forum*, Spring, 6–10.

Furunes T., Kaltveit A., & Akerjordet K. (2018). Health-promoting leadership: A qualitative study from experienced nurses' perspective. *Journal of Clinical Nursing*, 27, 4290–4301. https://doi.org/10.1111/jocn.14621

Goleman D. (2017). *Primal Leadership* (10th anniversary ed.). Harvard Business Review Press.

Hougaard, R., Carter, J., & Hobson, N. (2020, December 4). *Leadership & managing people. Compassionate leadership is necessary—but not sufficient.* Harvard Business Review. https://hbr.org/2020/12/compassionate-leadership-is-necessary-but-not-sufficient

Leclerc, L., Kennedy, K., & Campis, S. (2020). Human-centered leadership in healthcare: An idea that's time has come. *Nursing Administration Quarterly*, 44(2), 117–126.

Leclerc, L., Kennedy, K., & Campis, S. (2021). Human-centered leadership in healthcare: A contemporary nursing leadership theory generated via constructivist grounded theory. *Journal of Nursing Management*, 29, 294–306.

Porter-O'Grady T., & Malloch K. (2018). *Quantum leadership: Creating sustainable value in health care* (5th ed.). Jones & Bartlett Learning LLC.

Watson J. (2007). Caring theory as ethical guide to administrative and clinical practices. *Nursing Administration Quarterly*, 30(1), 48–55.

Watson J. (2009). Caring science and human caring theory: transforming personal and professional practices of nursing and health care. *Journal of Health and Human Services Administration*, 31(4), 466–482.

Williams, M., Penman, D., & Kabat-Zinn, J. (2012). *Mindfulness: An Eight-Week Plan for Finding Peace in a Frantic World.* Rodale Inc.

RECOMMENDED READING

Goulston, M., & Hendel, D. (2020). *Why cope when you can heal? How healthcare heroes of Covid-19 can recover from PTSD.* Harper Horizon.

Graham, L. (2013). *Bouncing back: Rewiring your brain for maximum resilience and well-being.* New World Library.

PART IV

DEVELOPING THE PEOPLE
WHO LEAD THE PEOPLE

Human-Centered Leaders require intentional development of skills that support the leader's effectiveness and the ability to create a sustainable culture of Excellence, Trust, and Caring. These skills, although not an exhaustive list, are briefly discussed in the following chapters.

Chapter 10

Emotional Intelligence: The Key to Human-Centered Leadership

"We delight in the beauty of the butterfly, but rarely admit the changes it has gone through to achieve that beauty."
—Maya Angelou, American Poet

By understanding one's own feelings, leaders can better understand and evaluate the feelings of others. This essential development is foundational to the Human-Centered Leader who understands *it starts with you, but it's not about you.*

I remember the first time I heard the term, "emotional intelligence." It was the late 90s. A PhD student in nursing sat before our nursing administration team with a stack of five or six heavy books to her right, one open in front of her, and enough engaging passion in her voice to fill up the entire room. She talked about the importance of emotional intelligence in every aspect of life and its significance in nursing. It was as if the abundance of her new knowledge and the excitement of "getting it out" to practicing nurse leaders could not be contained. It spewed out with urgent complexity. I was confused. I remember leaving the meeting with the realization that I had better quickly figure out what she was talking about or I would no doubt be left behind.

Through the years, I've studied and learned much more about the concept of emotional intelligence and even had the opportunity to teach it myself to doctoral students. It is one of the most valuable concepts to understand simply because it directly impacts your success in life. Travis Bradberry (2009), an expert in emotional intelligence, refers to it as "the way we manage behavior, navigate social complexities, and make personal decisions that achieve positive results" (p. 17).

We all know that Emotional Intelligence (often referred to as EQ) and Intellectual Quotient (IQ) are not related. IQ is your **ability to learn**, and it stays the same from the time you're roughly 15 to 50 years old. EQ, on the other hand, is a skill you can continue to improve upon throughout your life. According to Bradberry (2014), EQ is the "biggest predictor of performance in the workplace and the strongest driver of leadership and personal excellence" (p. 21). Bradberry goes on to say that the link between EQ and success in the workplace is so direct that each increased point of EQ correlates to an additional $1,300.00 in annual salary. Now that gets our attention!

Emotional Intelligence is made up of four components. Two of the components relate to **personal** competency and two relate to **social** competency. Personal competency includes self-awareness and self-management and relates to understanding and managing your own emotions. Social competency includes social awareness and relationship management and is about understanding other people's emotions and our ability to improve the quality of relationships. Refer to Figure 9 for defining characteristics of each of the components.

Emotional intelligence and Human-Centered Leadership fit together like a hand in glove. The match is intuitive when you consider the model called Emotional Intelligence Leadership, developed by Shankman and Allen (2008). They combined the concept of emotional intelligence with their knowledge of leadership and leadership development and included different leadership styles, aspects of organizational culture and behavior, positive psychology, and several other scholarly works in their model. Their simple, yet thorough, model includes three facets of leadership: consciousness of *self,* consciousness of *others,* and

Figure 9

The Four Components of Emotional Intelligence.

Personal Competency →	Self-Awareness	Self-Management
	• Reading your own emotions • Recognizing the impact of your emotions on yourself and others • Relying on your "gut-sense" to enhance decision-making • Knowing strengths and limitations • Having a sound sense of self-worth and knowing your capabilities	• Having emotional self-control • Being transparent • Being adaptable • Being achievement oriented • Taking initiative • Being optimistic
Social Competency →	Social Awareness	Relationship Management
	• Empathy—sensing others' emotions and understanding their perspective. Taking an interest in others' concerns • Organizational awareness—understanding decision networks and politics at the organizational level • Service—Recognizing and meeting the needs of followers, clients, and customers.	• Inspirational leadership • Influence • Developing others • Change catalyst • Conflict management • Building bonds • Teamwork/Collaboration

Note: Adapted from Bradberry, T., & Greaves, J. (2009). *Emotional intelligence 2.0.* TalentSmart; Goleman D. (2017). *Primal Leadership* (10th anniversary ed.). Harvard Business Review Press.

consciousness of *context* (Refer to Figure 10). While I will not explain Shankman and Allen's Emotional Intelligence Leadership model in detail, I will discuss the similarities between their model and Human-Centered Leadership as a way of emphasizing the necessity of emotional intelligence in Human-Centered Leadership.

Figure 10

Three core facets of emotionally intelligent leadership.

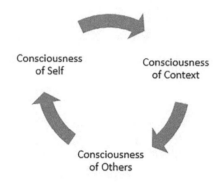

Note: The emotionally intelligent leader must be conscious of three fundamental facets of leadership: consciousness of self, others, and context. From Shankman, M. L., & Allen, S. (2008). *Emotionally intelligent leadership: A guide for college students.* Jossey-Bass.

Consciousness of Self—It starts with you!

The personal competencies associated with emotional intelligence are extremely important for the Human-Centered Leader who *starts with self*. Self-awareness and self-management are key components that we, as leaders, must consciously strive to develop. We discussed self-awareness in Chapter 3 and learned that it includes our ability to recognize, understand, and think about our emotions. In addition, it means knowing our blind spots, our strengths and weaknesses, and learning to be authentic.

Along with self-awareness, the Human-Centered Leader practices self-compassion, self-care, and mindfulness. Each of these practices contributes to our ability to manage our emotions—the other personal competency of emotional intelligence. Let's look at these practices individually and consider how they're connected to self-management.

In Chapter 5, we discussed how the practice of mindfulness increases our ability to choose to *respond* to intense emotions rather than *react*. In that split millisecond between the amygdala sensing danger, preparing us for fight or flight, and our left frontal cortex responding in a controlled and appropriate manner, we benefit from the neurological changes that mindfulness provides. Without the practice of mindfulness, it can be more difficult to tame the amygdala and manage our emotions.

Self-compassion also plays a role in managing our emotions. Think about how you could react or overreact to negative feedback if you're accustomed to constantly criticizing yourself. You may consider the negative feedback as confirmation that you're "not good enough" and become defeated, frustrated, or depressed. You may find it very difficult to bounce back from criticism. On the other hand, if you're accustomed to treating yourself with kindness, you're more readily able to accept negative feedback and apply a "can do" attitude toward improvement. You recognize that everyone makes mistakes, and you're no different. You're more optimistic and confident that you can make improvements and turn around a negative situation. You know you've bounced back before, and you will again.

Lastly, self-care also impacts our ability to manage emotions. Have you ever experienced a time when you consistently didn't get enough sleep? You manage fine until something happens, likely something small but out of your control, and you overreact. Maybe you snap at someone or maybe you tear up. Remember, sleep is considered one of the necessities in life and when the amygdala senses the ongoing stress of inadequate sleep and its impact on your body, it reacts and throws your emotions into high gear, making self-management much more difficult. By the way, the same thing happens when you're hungry!

Consciousness of self for the Human-Centered Leader means being aware of your emotions and managing your emotions through self-compassion, self-care, and mindfulness.

Consciousness of Others—It's not about you!

As you've learned, the Human-Centered Leader focuses outward through developing the leadership attributes of the Awakener, the Connector, and the

Upholder. This outward focus relies on the social competencies of emotional intelligence: social awareness and relationship management. As an Upholder, we must develop and practice **empathy** to form trusting relationships with our team and colleagues and to listen to and value others' perspectives. An "others-oriented mindset" enables us to recognize and meet the needs of staff and patients.

The traits of the Awakener and the Connector are consistent with the emotional intelligence required in the component of "Relationship Management." The Awakener is primarily focused on developing others while the Connector is embracing change, managing conflict, and bringing the team together.

Consciousness of others for the Human-Centered Leader means embodying the Upholder through empathy and service to others, the Awakener through development of others, and the Connector through bringing the team together.

Consciousness of Context—Culture is King!

Shankman and Allen (2008) expand on emotional intelligence to consider the importance of the context in which the leaders and followers work. They consider two components of context: *environmental awareness* and *group savvy.* The Human-Centered Leader's ultimate goal is a healthy culture, so we must be attuned to the environment, recognizing the positive aspects and any negative undertones. The Human-Centered Leader observes other leaders' interactions and reactions. Are leaders transparent about near misses? Do they truly want to know if someone is concerned about a possible safety issue? Do their actions match their words? How about the staff? Do they treat each other with respect, or do you see cliques and hear people gossiping in the breakroom? Is the staff highly valued by the executive leaders? Is it clear that quality and safe patient care are of ultimate importance? Do staff and leaders alike seek healthcare for their family members at their own organization? As you start to pay close attention to culture, you'll be able to spot the behaviors that contribute to excellence, trust, and caring. The critical metrics measuring patient and staff outcomes will confirm your findings (e.g. patient experience, staff satisfaction, staff turnover, "never" events, and readmission rates). Culture and outcomes track together, one reflecting the other.

Shankman and Allen (2008) also discuss the importance of *group savvy*. This requires the leader to pay attention to the different groups and the networking between groups and individuals within the organization. *Group savvy* can be described as "reading between the lines" when you're observing interactions. Which groups are the decision makers? Who speaks up and who listens? Who speaks up, yet no one listens? Do you sense any tension between groups? Given what you observe and learn, you're better positioned to negotiate, persuade, and influence the decision makers. You'll know which groups and individuals you must "win over" to support your position if you want to influence the entire organization.

A Human-Centered Leader has a keen eye for culture and employs *group savvy* to leverage influence among key players in the organization.

Emotional intelligence can be improved as we learn and grow as leaders. To thrive as a leader, we need a Human-Centered Leader who will provide mentoring and coaching so we will know our strengths but also our blind spots and limitations. You can be this leader for your followers as well. Embrace the practice of reflection, which you'll learn more about in Chapter 13, so that when you and your team members inevitably make mistakes, you'll be able to learn from them and improve your response when the next opportunity presents itself.

DISCUSSION QUESTIONS

1. Are there leaders in your organization who you consider to have a high level of emotional intelligence? What have you observed in their behavior that leads you to believe this?

2. In your opinion, which component of emotional intelligence is the most difficult to master and why? Are there opportunities to practice this specific skill in your daily work?

REFLECTION

Take an emotional assessment quiz to get an idea of your strengths and areas for growth. You can take any number of available online quizzes or the assessment provided with *Emotional Intelligence 2.0* by Bradberry and Greaves. You can find a simple 15-question quiz called "How emotionally intelligent are you?" on the Mind Tools website.

1. What are your areas of strength?
2. What are your areas for growth?
3. Which component would you like to improve?
4. Reflect and commit to one strategy you can put in place to take a step towards improving your EI.

_____

_____

_____

_____

_____

REFERENCES

Bradberry, T. (2014, January 9). *Emotional Intelligence—EQ.* Forbes. https://www.forbes.com/sites/travisbradberry/2014/01/09/emotional-intelligence/?sh=374c10e11ac0

Bradberry, T., & Greaves, J. (2009). *Emotional intelligence 2.0.* TalentSmart.

Goleman, D., Boyatzis, R., & McKee, A. (2013). *Primal leadership: Unleashing the power of emotional intelligence.* Harvard Business Review Press.

Shankman, M. L., & Allen, S. (2008). *Emotionally intelligent leadership: A guide for college students.* Jossey-Bass.

RECOMMENDED READING

Goleman, D. (2000). *Working with emotional intelligence.* Random House Publishing Group.

Stein, S. J., & Howard, E. (2011). *The EQ edge: Emotional intelligence and your success* (3rd edition). Jossey-Bass.

Chapter 11

Change Management: Expect the Unexpected!

"It is not the strongest or the most intelligent who will survive but those who can best manage change."
—**Charles Darwin**, English Naturalist and Scientist

B en Franklin, one of the founding fathers of the United States, is famous for a 1789 quote, "In this world nothing can be said to be certain, except death and taxes." We would amend that quote and add "change." Nothing is more certain in our current 21st century world than the expectation that change is to be anticipated and constant. As a Human-Centered Leader working in a complex healthcare world whose primary business product centers on complex human beings, change is part of every waking moment. Our patients, teams, and colleagues are gifted with free will, which is the ability to make choices about their everyday world. In healthcare, we generally consider this a form of autonomy. For patients, it's the right to decide what they will or will not accept about their care. For nurses or healthcare team members, autonomy is deciding what we will or will not accept about our work environment (ANA, 2015). Sounds like a lot of humans making a lot of decisions. What we expect to happen in the course of our day is influenced by all these decisions. Consider this example to illustrate: You're a primary care nurse working on a busy unit caring for five patients along with their family members, physicians, patient care technicians, dieticians, and so on. How often do you think your day will go as expected? I think we all know the answer is probably an indisputable "never." Most nurses are masters of change management, whether they recognize it or not. We adapt to our patients' changing symptoms, better or worse, with critical thinking and actions. We negotiate meals with hungry, often "hangry," patients. We become the family's connection to transitions in care. We guide the care team through daily adjustments in scheduling labs, tests, and consults. We also navigate working alongside colleagues, physicians, charge nurses, and nurse managers. I'm tired just thinking about all those decision points in one day. Are all nurses open to change? Of course not. Most of us have worked with nursing teams long enough to know there will be a healthy mix of personalities. We always have the nurses who like to be change-makers, the "glass is half full" people, and we always have some change resisters, the "glass is half empty" people. In nursing, the Human-Centered Leader recognizes the opportunity to harness the energy from both types of nurses. The balance lies in the creative and innovative ideas of the "sky is the limit" people with the reality check of barriers provided by the "we like it this way" people. In this chapter, we'll review techniques and tools for how the Human-Centered Leader can manage change, big or small.

Do any of these names for change management sound familiar? PDSA? Kotter? Lewin? Rogers? ADKAR? Lean? Did you know the nursing process is a change model? That's right, assessment, diagnosis, planning, implementation, and evaluation is a change-management process. What all these models have in common is the linear and problem-focused nature of the method. For example, first, we identify the problem. Then we do "A," then "B" and hopefully "C" will unfold as the outcome or expected change. Does this always happen? Anyone who's ever worked in healthcare knows the resounding answer to this question is "no!" As we mentioned earlier, we deal with humans in all their glorious complexity and free will. This means linear and problem-centered change models don't reliably produce consistent outcomes. In other words, despite our best efforts to treat and care for our patients, complex humans often don't respond the way we would like them to. As a change framework, problem-focused thinking can create fragmentation among staff, limit visions of positive potential change, perpetuate negative feedback cycles that are unfulfilling, and lead to "problem fatigue" caused by a consistent focus on deficits rather than possibilities. The good news is that there are also nonlinear, non-deficit ways of approaching change which we'll discuss next: complexity/chaos and appreciative inquiry. Because linear, problem-centric approaches are common in healthcare, effective leaders can decide which linear and nonlinear approaches are most appropriate based on the situation, the problem, and the people involved. Regardless of where you work in healthcare, change management is part of your life.

Nonlinear Change Management

Think Like an Edgewalker: Complexity, Chaos, and the Human-Centered Leader

Do you ever wonder why things can't just stay the same? Why is that our workday rarely turns out the same as yesterday? It's those complex humans again, and I don't just mean the patients. Often, our colleagues and everyone on the team bring unique challenges and complexity to our day. According to Porter-O'Grady and Malloch (2018), dynamic environments, such as those we see in healthcare, make chaos visible because it pushes systems to forever adapt to changes in the environment. Traditional approaches to leadership try to mitigate or prevent the unpredictable, whereas a Human-Centered Leader embraces the idea that change, the unexpected, and the subsequent consequences, which may include conflict, are much closer to the reality we face each day. As a Human-Centered Leader, we can develop and integrate concepts of change management in terms that are congruent with a complex system. First, we should aim to shift our thinking to see chaos as the edge of change, not as the day gone haywire. Chaos and order are opposites and often occur at the same time. Being able to "see" the chaos for what it is helps us balance the constant dance between stimulus and response. Luckily, we can choose how we respond. Using mindfulness and an in-the-moment pause also allows us to stop being reactive to situations. Remember that the Connector and the Awakener in our Human-Centered selves recognizes turbulence or chaos as the space where momentum is gained. It's the space where we have a great opportunity to adapt to a new way of being. In particular, the Connector's aim to facilitate the voice of edgewalkers within the team is integral to managing change in terms of chaos. The edgewalker embraces change and chaos by endorsing experimentation with ideas to generate innovation within a safe environment. In summary, consider the following case example and tools for managing chaos and complexity:

Case: You're the assistant nurse manager in the emergency department (ED) on the 3:00 p.m.–11:00 p.m. shift. Throughput is slow with a backlog of ED holds because beds aren't available on the medical-surgical unit. Your nurses are overloaded and frustrated. You're worried about safe patient care.

1. **Change your mindset to expect the unexpected.**

    Your response: Check in with yourself and realize your expectation for throughput is influenced by the complexity of the system. As a Human-Centered Leader, you realize the ED is inextricably connected to the throughput on the medical-surgical unit. There are variables causing unexpected challenges in your world. Change your mindset to see this as a normal challenge.

2. **Recognize the complexity of your teams, patients, and colleagues** (remember free will!).

    Your response: Keep in mind your ED and the medical-surgical unit are complex adaptive systems reliant on human responses and organizational processes. You choose to reach out to your counterpart on the unit and see what's going on. When you discover the unit is down one nurse and housekeeping had two callouts this evening, you discover the foundation for the delayed discharges and turnover to clean beds.

3. **Stop being reactive to change and instead aim to dance with the chaos. Choose your response.**

    Your response: Consider how you might facilitate patient flow from your perspective. Can you spare a patient-care tech to assist on the unit with discharges? Can you, yourself, go to the unit to help?

4. **Develop an awareness that chaos is really the edge of change.**

Your response: While you're on the way to the unit to help with discharges and turning over the rooms, you realize the current chaos is an opportunity to change a number of things. First, by reaching out to be present on the unit, you're extending trust and taking the first step to show collaboration between two historically contentious teams. Second, you're modeling teamwork and mutual collaboration. While walking up to the unit, you plan to talk with your manager about an idea to "Walk a Mile in My Shoes." It hits you that you don't know much about how the unit works, and they certainly don't know much about how the ED works.

5. **Instead of guessing or filling in the story, ask patients or teams about potential causes of chaos, i.e., staffing, lack of resources.**

   Your response: Instead of making the usual assumptions that the nurses on the unit are intentionally slowing the discharge process to avoid admissions, you choose to discover what's really going on. You stop the voice in your head telling a story of your own making. You find out the real story, which involves staffing issues, and when you get to the unit, you see just how short-staffed and overrun the nurses and assistants are. You now respond with empathy and teamwork, rather than judgment.

6. **Create a safe space to allow "edgewalking" and experimentation of ideas to generate innovation.**

   Your response: Recognize the model you create when you respond to chaos with calm, thoughtful, and intentional ideas and actions. Your edgewalking will generate the same spirit of innovation in your team and, perhaps, the medical-surgical nurses. Your "Walk a Mile in My Shoes" idea will benefit the teams in both the ED and the unit and, of course, the patients.

Appreciative Inquiry

Do you ever get tired of huddles and visual management boards that seem to always focus on what you're doing wrong? What if there was a way to flip the script and focus on what you and your colleagues are doing well in an effort to reach a goal? What if we approached our goals and the oh-so-famous metrics with "possibility" thinking rather than "deficit" thinking? Imagine your daily huddles around the visual management board being led with questions to build on strengths, generate positive energy, and encourage creativity. Imagine being asked rather than told how to approach the problem. This is what appreciative inquiry is all about. According to David Cooperrider (2020), renowned organizational behaviorist and researcher, appreciative inquiry is a change theory designed to engage stakeholders in self-identified transformation. Appreciative inquiry differs from traditional change theories because rather than focusing on a problem or deficiency as a foundation for change, appreciative inquiry focuses on current strengths and what's working well in an organization or entity. The beauty of appreciative inquiry is best described by one of its most prolific organizational theorists, Dr. Gervase Bushe (2012), who provided an eloquent description shared below.

Appreciative Inquiry advocates collective inquiry into the best of what is, in order to imagine what could be, followed by collective design of a desired future state that is compelling, and thus, does not require the use of incentives, coercion, or persuasion for planned change to occur (Bushe, 2012, p. 93).

Appreciative Inquiry aligns with the Human-Centered Leader's duty to seek out and listen to the voice of team members and patients (Connector and Awakener). Appreciative inquiry is based on an assumption that the questions we ask will lead us in a particular direction and change will occur parallel to the questions we pursue most persistently and passionately. This exemplifies the Human-Centered Leader's inner Connector, who aims to build community through collaboration, support, edgewalking, engineering, and authentic communication. Appreciative inquiry is not just a positive way to approach change, it's transformational because it's a collective effort and hinges on the creative generation of new ideas to address old problems. Sounds a lot like shared governance, doesn't it? In its simplest form, the Human-Centered Leader uses appreciative inquiry to allow those at the epicenter of the problem to discover, dream, design, and deliver transformational and positive change (Leclerc, 2017). In summary, here are the steps, along with an example of how the Human-Centered Leader can use appreciative inquiry with individuals, teams, and colleagues. Try it yourself one day soon in a huddle or staff meeting.

Case: During your medical-surgical unit's monthly staff meeting, you, the nurse manager, facilitate a conversation about length of stay. Your aim is to use appreciative inquiry to generate ideas around change management that might influence the trending increase in length of stay.

1. **Define:** What is the topic and *focus for change*? Clarify the work to be done.

   Example: Length of stay has been steadily rising on your medical-surgical unit due to patients not being ambulated regularly before the day of discharge.

2. **Discover:** Appreciate, rediscover, and remember the *best of what is*. What's working well in current system? Or what worked well in the past?

   Example: One of the nurses highlights the value of dedicated "turn teams" from a previous hospital he worked at; a nursing assistant speaks up and says she's familiar with the concept as well, and it worked to help keep patients from being entirely sedentary.

3. **Dream:** Imagine *what could be*. Dare your team to envision the future based on their best and wildest dreams.

   Example: After some assurance from you that they can dream freely, your team says they would love to have dedicated "stroll patrols" for every four-hour rounds with patients who need to get up and walk; one nurse suggests a "parade" of patients to energize and encourage the patients.

4. **Design:** Determine *what should be* through merging the stories from "discovery" with the imagination and creativity from "the dream."

   Example: You, the nurses, and the nursing assistants work through the logistics of merging both ideas within current staffing models and interdisciplinary rounding schedules.

5. **Deliver/Destiny:** Create *what will be.* Develop a collaborative, structured, and thoughtful plan for implementation that realizes the destiny of the team's ideas.

   Example: It's decided to pilot Stroll Patrols at 11:00 a.m. and 2:00 p.m. to work through the logistics. The patrol will be comprised of an RN and nursing assistant caring for the same patients. Patients with anticipated discharge within one to two days will be prioritized.

Linear Change Management

Remember all those change-management models mentioned at the beginning of this chapter? If we had more time, we could get nostalgic about "way back in the day" when PDSA was the "innovative" way to implement the next new thing on the unit. We could also reminisce about our nursing school days when we learned about the nursing process. Although all the linear change models listed in Table 12 are effective, we're challenging you to consider merging concepts from linear and nonlinear change methods to better address the complexity that exists in our everyday world of healthcare. In light of that, keep in mind your organization might also have a prevailing change method that's preferred or even expected, e.g., Lean or Lean Six Sigma. Our recommendation is to honor the prevailing method of your organization but be creative and innovative by infusing concepts of appreciative inquiry or complexity change management to complement your efforts.

Table 12

Linear Change Models

Change Model	Summary	Steps	Founder/Author
Nursing Process	Traditional five-step approach to short- and long-term goals in patient care.	• Assessment • Planning • Diagnosis • Implementation • Evaluation	Orlando, I. J. (1961). *The dynamic nurse-patient relationship.* Putnam's Sons.

PDSA	Primary intention is to develop a cyclical proposal to test a proposed change.	• Plan • Do • Study • Act	Deming, W.E. (1986). *Out of the crisis*. MIT Press.

Lean	Model based on cost reduction and reducing waste. Primary premise is that cost reduction through process change will increase efficiency.	• Insights
		• Options (cost, value, impact)
		• Experiments
		  o Prepare
		  o Introduce
		  o Review
			Multiple authors and developers: Kiichiro Toyota—early 1900s Henry Ford—early 1900s Taichi Ohno—1950s Shiegeo Shingo—1960s Kaizen Source: Hessing, T. (2019). *History of Lean*. Six Sigma Study Guide. https://sixsigmastudyguide.com history-of-lean/

Lewin's 3-Stage Model of Change	Three-step change process designed for utility at micro- and macro-level systems. Focuses on better understanding driving and restraining forces.	• Unfreezing • Movement • Freezing	Lewin, K. (1951). *Field theory in social sciences*. Harper & Row.

Kotter's Change Management Model	Developed with unique aspect to anticipate resistance from employees and proactively develop a plan to address. Focuses on employees' responses to change.	• Increase urgency • Build a guiding coalition • Form a strategic vision • Enlist a volunteer army • Enable action by removing barriers • Generate short-term wins • Sustain acceleration • Institute change	Kotter, J. P. (2012). *Leading change.* Harvard Business Review Press.
McKinsey 7-S Framework	Describes the seven stages through which a company must progress when implementing a set of changes. Focuses on diverse stakeholders or entities that may be impacted by the change.	• Structure • Systems • Skills • Staff • Strategy • Shared Values	1980s McKinsey consultants: Tom Peters, Robert Waterman & Julien Philips.
ADKAR Model	Recognizes the need for small, incremental changes over time. Changes are orderly and moderate, so employees have a chance to adapt before the next wave of changes strikes.	• Awareness of need for change • Desire to make change • Knowledge of strategic vision • Ability to enforce change • Reinforcement to instill long-term change	Hiatt, J. M. (2006). *ADKAR: A model for change in business, government and our community.* Prosci Learning Center Publications.

Rogers' Diffusion of Innovation	Five-step process explaining how, why, and at what rate new ideas are adopted by individuals.	• Knowledge • Persuasion • Decision • Implementation • Confirmation	Rogers, E. (1995). *Diffusion of innovations* (4th ed.). Free Press.

Nonlinear, Linear, or Both: Be the Change!

Entire books have been written and dedicated to change management. The intention of the content provided here is to remind us of techniques that have worked in the past and, perhaps, introduce some new ways of thinking, i.e., appreciative inquiry and complexity-based change management. Keep in mind, as complex humans leading complex humans, we'll rarely use one single technique or approach for managing change. Often, based on the situation, we must deftly integrate multiple perspectives and methods. Remember, we encourage you to use your organization's preferred structure, but consider creative or alternate ways to engage the team that can parallel that structure. As you embrace your inner Upholder, you'll become practiced at managing change with an *organizationally aware* approach that aligns the team's passion and creativity with the hospital's goals. The Connector in you will create the safe space for *edgewalking* through *support* and *engineering* of shared decision-making and shared leadership. You will allow your team to dream! Finally, the Awakener in you will *coach* and *mentor* by focusing on positive rather than deficit-based change management. Effective coaches and mentors are able to help the team see the potential excellence that lies within each person. As a Human-Centered Leader you then create the empowering environment that allows the team to link their internal motivation to the benefits of change such as improved patient outcomes and a healthier work environment.

DISCUSSION QUESTIONS

1. Read this quote by John Lewis, a United States Senator and civil rights activist who enjoyed getting in "good trouble" and facilitating change:
   "Take a long, hard look down the road you will have to travel once you have made a commitment to work for change. Know that this

transformation will not happen right away. Change often takes time. It rarely happens all at once."

a. What is one change you believe needs to happen within your department or unit that might take a good bit of time, i.e., three to six months or longer?

b. Which change model would be most appropriate? Linear, nonlinear, or a mix of both?

2. When thinking about your organization, which change-management model is most frequently used or recommended? How effective has it been in creating sustained change? Outcomes?

REFLECTION

Think about the Appreciative Inquiry process to Define, Discover, Dream, Design, and Deliver/Destiny. How do you feel this change process aligns with your leadership style? Do you currently focus on deficits or problems? Or do you tend to take what's working well and build on it to foster innovation with team members at the center of the decision?

_____

_____

_____

_____

_____

_____

REFERENCES

American Nurses Association. (2015). *Code of ethics for nurses with interpretive statements.* https://www.nursingworld.org/practice-policy/nursing-excellence/ethics/code-of-ethics-for-nurses/

Bushe, G. R. (2012). Appreciative inquiry: theory and critique. In D. Boje, B. Burnes, & J. Hassard (Eds.), *The Routledge Companion to Organizational Change* (pp. 87-103). Routledge.

Cooperrider, D. (2020). *5-D cycle of appreciative inquiry*. The Appreciative Inquiry Commons. https://appreciativeinquiry.champlain.edu/learn/appreciative-inquiry-introduction/5-d-cycle-appreciative-inquiry/

Deming, W. E. (1986). *Out of the crisis*. MIT Press.

Hessing, T. (2019). *History of Lean*. Six Sigma Study Guide. https://sixsigmastudyguide.com/history-of-lean/

Hiatt, J. M. (2006). *ADKAR: A model for change in business, government and our community*. Prosci Learning Center Publications.

Kotter, J. P. (2012). *Leading change*. Harvard Business Review Press.

Lewin, K. (1951). *Field theory in social sciences*. Harper & Row.

Leclerc, L. (2017). The journey of 10,000 miles begins with one step. *Nurse Leader*, 15(4), 266-270. https://doi.org/10.1016/j.mnl.2017.03.015

Orlando, I. J. (1961). *The dynamic nurse-patient relationship*. Putnam's Sons.

Rogers, E. (1995). *Diffusion of innovations* (4th ed.). Free Press.

RECOMMENDED READING

Cooperrider, D. L, Sorensen, P. F., Jr., Yaeger, T. F., & Whitney, D. (2001). *Appreciative inquiry: An emerging direction for organization development*. Stipes Publishing.

Cooperrider, D. L., Whitney, D., & Stavros, J. M. (2003). *Appreciative inquiry handbook*. Lakeshore Publisher.

Gholipour, B. (2019, March 21). Philosophers and neuroscientists join forces to see whether science can solve the mystery of free will. *Science*. https://doi:10.1126/science.aax4190

Wagner, J. (Ed.). (2018). *Leadership and influencing change in nursing*. UR Press. https://ourspace.uregina.ca/handle/10294/8296.

Chapter 12

Connecting the Three Cs: Competence, Capability, and Complexity

"Success occurs when opportunity meets preparation."
—**Zig Ziglar**, American Author and Inspirational Speaker

Rather than primarily focusing on "competencies," Human-Centered Leaders focus on "capabilities." The leader must practice reflection and develop critical thinking to build and model capability.

"The Year of the Nurse and Midwife," which was designated by the World Health Organization (WHO) in 2020, shined a bright light on the significance, value, trust, and praise the public held for bedside nurses while our entire world faced the challenges brought on by COVID-19. With their special 2020 designation, the WHO intended to advance the vital position of nurses and midwives in transforming healthcare around the world. This noble intent continues to manifest as nurses collaborate with other professionals to navigate the complexity made visible through the pandemic. COVID-19 provided the opportunity for the world to experience together the complexity of healthcare, industry, education, and economics. Until then, complexity for many of us was an underlying concept or theory; something to "consider" rather than to "live." Once complexity theory became a visible reality, healthcare professionals recognized the need to be prepared for chaos, embrace unpredictability, leverage collaboration, create, innovate, and grasp the interconnectedness of systems. Now that we know what is needed to thrive in a complex environment, how can nurse educators and nurse leaders better prepare nurses to lead and practice in a way that transforms healthcare?

Preparing for Complexity

Traditionally, education of nurses has focused on the development and demonstration of specific competencies. As nurses, we are familiar with basic competencies required for new nurses entering practice, competencies required at the end of orientation, and then ongoing competencies required for continued practice. These competencies help ensure the standardization of tasks and safe patient care. While knowledge and skill validation through the performance of competencies is a minimum requirement for practice, how do we go beyond competency to prepare and engage nurses to meet the inherent complexity of healthcare? Will competency alone take nurses to the edge of chaos where solutions are created? What personal characteristics should be encouraged and modeled by nurse leaders? What types of learning activities result in the nurse's ability to embrace change, take risks, learn from mistakes, and develop creative innovations? Are nurses being prepared to practice in changing contexts and work collaboratively with other healthcare professionals to work collaboratively to develop solutions? Nurse educators and nurse leaders must focus on these things.

Difference Between Competency and Capability

Competency and capability differ in that capability builds on competency and embraces complexity. You may have to think about that for a minute! Fraser and Greenhalgh (2001) define *competence* as "what individuals know and are able to do in terms of knowledge, skills, and attitude" (p. 799). On the other hand, *capability* is the "extent to which individuals can adapt to change, generate new knowledge, and continue to improve their performance" (p. 799). So, if we stop at competency, we are not fulfilling our individual potential or meeting the requirements to thrive in a complex system.

Awakening Capability

In the Human-Centered Leadership model, the leader, as an Awakener, models continuous, life-long learning and a focus on learning and growing as inherent to the nursing profession. The nurses connect their daily work to their overall professional goals and purpose by using their individual growth plans as a guide. Their internal motivation is enhanced by the Awakener's mentoring and coaching. The Awakener ensures a learning environment by encouraging appropriate experimentation with problem-solving and embracing the reflective practice of learning from mistakes. By constructing the NPG council to facilitate staff participation in decision-making and to advocate for the needs of the team, the Awakener demonstrates that a learning environment is transformational for the staff.

Fraser & Greenhalgh (2001) suggest techniques to enhance capability through nonlinear teaching methods such as storytelling and small group, problem-based learning. We all know that meaningful stories are more memorable than facts. I'll never forget a story I heard from a young lady named Carey, who shared her personal experiences as a patient in the ICU. As an ICU nurse, I've always wondered what that experience was like for a patient. I had hoped that they didn't remember the pain, the intrusive equipment, or the constant alarms. Because of my interest, I was on the edge of my chair with anticipation after Carey was introduced at the end of the TeamStepps course I was attending. The course focused on the impact of teams working together to ensure safe patient care and culminated with Carey's story. Carey was currently working as a patient advocate at a large teaching hospital, using her personal experiences as a patient to improve the experiences of other patients. She described how her disease process had caused her to be intubated numerous times. She began by telling us about her first intubation and what her experience was like. I expected her to describe in detail the pain of an endotracheal tube, the anxiety associated with suctioning or weaning, and the horrible sensations of air hunger or drowning. She may have covered this to some degree, but what I remember most is her description of how it felt to be treated as someone who couldn't hear because she couldn't speak. The care team gathered at her bedside and talked over her, or worse, they gathered outside the door to discuss her care. She wasn't a part of the team. Her thoughts didn't seem to matter. She didn't feel like the decision-maker in her own care. She felt "less than" a person. I remember crying as she described these feelings in detail, wondering how many of my patients had experienced the same feelings. Fortunately, her experiences improved, and she went on to describe the conversations and agreements she made with her care team on subsequent visits to the ICU. Remember, she had been intubated numerous times. Carey insisted, and the care team agreed, that she was to be a part of her care; in fact, she would be at the *center* of her care. Carey talked of subsequent hospitalizations when she was intubated, how she would sit up in the bed when the care team rounded and communicate using different codes, gestures, and body language. Nothing happened without her agreement. Hearing Carey's story taught me what patient-centered care in the ICU looked like and the value of including the patient as a member of the care team. Her story made me a better nurse. It connected me to my purpose and my desire to do things differently. I guess you could say my paradigm shifted, and I saw patient-centered care differently from that point on. I was capable of more than I had been capable of before.

Other experiences with multi-professional, problem-based learning groups have impacted me in similar ways. One memorable case study was presented by an interventional cardiologist and engaging teacher, Dr. Brooks. He would gather a team of physicians, ICU nurses, floor nurses, and cardiac catheterization lab techs together every month and offer a case study for our learning. He engaged our creativity and problem-solving skills as we considered cases that crossed all areas of the hospital. Each person's thoughts were as highly valued as the next, and the fact that there was a mix of different professionals within the group only made for richer learning.

I remember one very intriguing case study that he titled, *Starry Night,* after Van Gogh's famous painting. Dr. Brooks told us that he hoped the painting would engage our creative sides. He then began introducing the case study. A 55-year-old male patient presented to his office with palpitations and a slow, irregular heartbeat. The patient had a list of other symptoms as well: nausea, vomiting, dizziness, some changes in vision, and headache. We looked at the EKGs and the echocardiogram. We talked about the fact that the patient's gastrointestinal symptoms and possible neurological symptoms were puzzling given his primary cardiac problem. Were they connected or separate issues? Dr. Brooks presented one clue after the next until finally he shared the patient's list of medications. There on the list was digoxin, a cardiac medication used for heart failure. As you probably know, digoxin is a very potent medication, and a small dose of 0.125–0.25 mg is typically prescribed. This patient's dose, however, was considered high at 0.50 mg. The pieces of the puzzle were starting to come together. After more conversation, the team realized that the patient had digitalis toxicity, which explained every one of his symptoms. But what did this have to do with Van Gogh's painting, *Starry Night*? Dr. Brooks went on to share a couple other paintings by Van Gogh. There was one of Van Gogh's doctor, Dr. Gachet, who was seated at a desk and holding a wilted long-stemmed flower called foxglove. We also looked at Van Gogh's self-portrait in which one pupil was larger than the other. The yellow swirly haze around the stars, the foxglove plant from which digitalis is derived, and the neurological symptom of unequal pupils provided the clues for a cumulative "aha" moment. Clearly, Dr. Brooks' patient wasn't the only one with digitalis toxicity! I feel sure the entire group of caregivers and care providers in that classroom never forgot the symptoms of digitalis toxicity. We learned the value of considering every detail when determining a diagnosis. We learned specifically about the effects of digitalis toxicity through the nonlinear methods of storytelling and multi-professional, group problem-solving. We also shared the experience of appreciating a master's fine art.

Process-Oriented Learning Methods

Fraser and Greenhalgh (2001) describe the need for process-oriented learning methods. We can all relate to the methods that work best for adult learners. We typically like to learn on an "as needed" basis. We enjoy working with mentors or peer groups, but we also need time to reflect and study. We appreciate working in small groups because we often achieve more together than we would as individuals. Did you know that this small-group approach reflects a nonlinear effect in a complex system? It's because social interactions stimulate learning and increase team members' confidence and motivation (2001).

Below, Table 13, is a list of process-oriented learning methods provided by Fraser and Greenhalgh (2001, pg. 802).

Table 13

Process-Oriented Learning

Informal and Unplanned Learning
• Experimental learning—shadowing, apprenticeships
• Networking opportunities
• Learning activities—reflection, group discussion
• "Buzz groups"—quick connections with a peer during breaks in a lecture
• Teach-back opportunities
• Feedback—providing projected outcomes of actions
Self-Directed Learning
• Mentoring
• Peer-supported learning groups
• Personal learning log—identifying new learning needs
• Appraisal—assessing progress towards goals
Nonlinear learning
• Case-based discussions
• Simulations
• Role play
• Small group, problem-based learning
• Teambuilding exercises

Note: Adapted from Fraser, S. W., & Greenhalgh, T. (2001). Coping with complexity: Educating for capability. *British Medical Association*, 323, 799–803.

What Does a Capable Nurse Look Like? Creative, has a high degree of self-efficacy, knows how to learn, can take appropriate and effective action to formulate and solve problems, can apply competencies in unfamiliar and familiar situations, works well with others (Cairns, 2000; O'Connell et al., 2014)

Strive for Competence and Capability

As nurse leaders and nurse educators, we must prepare nurses to *thrive* in a complex environment if we are to *drive* the transformation of healthcare around the world. Frontline nurse leaders, who were likely promoted for their outstanding clinical care, become the leaders best positioned to influence outcomes at the point of care. These influential leaders must not be left to their own self-taught knowledge. Instead, they must be intentionally developed in ways that stretch them to become capable leaders who embrace unpredictability with flexibility, creativity, and confidence. This approach to development requires both linear and nonlinear learning and enables the nurse leader to apply learning in constantly changing and challenging environments.

Human-Centered Leadership in Healthcare provides a model for nurse leaders to become resilient and capable. Leaders start by focusing inward to establish the "self" practices that build resiliency. From that vantage point, nurse leaders turn their attention outward to their staff, who care for the patients. It's through awakening, connecting, and upholding their staff that Human-Centered Leaders are able to have a nonlinear effect and create a positive culture. This is a different, process-oriented approach to *develop the people who lead the people who care for the people.*

DISCUSSION QUESTIONS

1. What teaching strategies are used at your school or healthcare organization to help prepare nurses for the complexity of healthcare?

2. What current problem are you experiencing that a multi-professional, problem-based group could tackle? Remember it's not a coincidence when a small group is more innovative than individuals, it's the reality of complexity!

3. Think about the team you lead and the ways they have adapted to change. Discuss ways that you can further develop them and appreciate them for their capabilities.

REFLECTION

Think back over the last few years and reflect on a learning opportunity that was significant in your development as a nurse leader. What did you learn and what impact has this learning had on you?

_____

_____

_____

_____

_____

_____

REFERENCES

Cairns, L. (2000). *The process/outcomes approach to becoming a capable organization*. Australian Capability Network Conference, Sydney.

Fraser, S. W., & Greenhalgh, T. (2001). Coping with complexity: Educating for capability. *British Medical Association, 323*, 799–803.

O'Connell, J., Gardner, G., & Coyer, F. (2014). Beyond competencies: Using a capability framework in developing practice standards for advanced practice nursing. *Journal of Advanced Nursing, 70*(12), 2728–2735.

RECOMMENDED READING

Berger, J.G. (2019). *Unlocking leadership mindtraps: How to thrive in complexity*. Stanford University Press.

Clifton, J., & Harter, J. (2019). *It's the manager: Gallup finds that the quality of managers and team leaders is the single biggest factor in your organization's long-term success*. Gallup Press.

Schein, E. & Schein, P. A. (2018). *Humble leadership: The power of relationships, openness, and trust*. Berrett-Koehler Publishers.

Chapter 13

Reflective Practice: Learning from Experience

"We do not learn from the experience, we learn from reflecting on the experience."

—**John Dewey**, American Philosopher, Educator, and Psychologist

T he Human-Centered Leader fosters a deeper learning gained by reflecting on experiences. By practicing and teaching reflection, the leader fosters lifetime learning for both self and others.

The Human-Centered Leader understands personal and professional success starts with personal well-being, which includes self care, self compassion, and self-awareness. (Leclerc et. al., 2020). Self-awareness is the ability to look deep within yourself, and, in an honest and authentic manner, identify and acknowledge your thoughts, emotions, beliefs, and intentions. Becoming a truly self-aware person requires commitment, open mindedness, and self-reflection. Many of us spend some part of our day assessing and reflecting on experiences or events that have occurred. For many people, personal reflection is a natural and instinctive exercise, and is viewed as a necessary and relevant tool used to strengthen self-awareness, develop self-compassion, and promote mindfulness. We examine our thoughts, behaviors, and actions around our experiences in an effort to enhance personal growth and development. The great philosopher, Confucius, highlighted the importance of reflection when he stated, "Learning without reflection is a waste, reflection without learning is dangerous." His teachings explain the strong connection between reflection and gaining knowledge. When we reflect on what we have learned through our experiences and then apply the new knowledge, or lessons learned, to what we already know, personal and professional growth and development will follow.

When I was an adolescent, struggling with all of the adolescent angst experienced during this period, a very wise woman—my mom—suggested I start a diary to write down my thoughts and feelings. I remember my first diary. It was the size of a small book. It had a colorful picture of a kitten on the front, and it had a key that I kept hidden in a shoe in my closet. I viewed my diary as something intensely personal, private, and almost sacred. When I first started writing in my diary, I found myself staring at an empty white page, wondering what in the world to write about. My earliest entries included a summary of my day: what I ate, what I did, and who I had interacted with. My entries were basic, straightforward, and, honestly, kind of boring. As time progressed however, my diary entries became more reflective and personal. I began to write down the lyrics to songs I liked, copy inspirational quotes that spoke to me, and review books I was reading. Slowly but surely, I found myself becoming more reflective about experiences and events. I began recording thoughts and feelings about things going on in my world, thinking about my behavior and identifying lessons learned. As I became more comfortable with journaling, I began reflecting on my values, beliefs, and my purpose in the world. The process of reflecting on my experiences and then writing them down started me on the journey of self-discovery. I began to identify my strengths and weaknesses. I was able to release emotions and frustrations that seemed to weigh me down. I identified personal goals, dreams, and ideas. I began to better understand my purpose and my passions. The dynamic act of journaling was a way to reflect on the experiences occurring in my life, and to gain insight into the emotions, thoughts, and behaviors surrounding those experiences.

Self-reflection has become the springboard for the more modern professional concept of reflective practice. Reflective practice is an adaptable and effective methodology, using insights and past experiences to steer both future personal and professional growth and development. This methodology serves as a tool through which people can gain knowledge by deliberately reflecting on an experience and identifying the thoughts, emotions, and actions surrounding the experience. Reflective practice asks challenging questions related to how we think and feel about ourselves in relation to our experiences. It's been described as an approach that encourages us to use insights and lessons learned from our past to help assess our current position. In doing this, we help to improve both our present and our future by integrating activities into our life that raise awareness, support decision-making, and prompt critical thinking. Reflective practice encompasses the art of learning to pay attention by listening and observing ourselves, as well as recognizing and identifying any assumptions we might have. Reflective practice is also noticing habits and patterns, acknowledging what we see, and, in some instances, committing to change the way we see it. It's tough personal work and sometimes can require "tough skin," but a strong reflective practice can be an effective tool for self-empowerment. Within this chapter, we will cover several models and tools for your practical use in the day-to-day work of professional and personal reflection.

Cultivating a Reflective Mindset

The practice of reflecting on events and experiences, focusing on our reactions and feelings, is the foundation for self-awareness. Developing insights and strategies based on our reflective practice is the model for professional growth. Embracing a reflective practice supports us in the journey to understand and learn from our experiences. Understanding what we learned and why we learned it helps link us to our "bigger picture." In other words, reflective practice deepens personal and professional growth and learning by providing a tool to help us objectively recognize and articulate lessons learned. So how do you become a reflective practitioner?

Donald Schon, philosopher, author, and expert on reflective practice, describes the first stage as cultivating the skills to reflect critically on your past experiences (Smith, 2001/2011). He calls this process **Reflection *on* Action**, and defines it in four stages: *Re-inhabit*, or relive the experience; *Reflect* on the experience, noticing and acknowledging what was happening; *Review* the experience, critically analyzing the moment; and finally, *Reframe* the experience by coming to a new and perhaps more insightful understanding. Schon calls the second stage of reflective practice the **Reflection *in* Action**, more commonly known as the ability to "think on your feet." This stage involves reflecting on an experience or situation as it is occurring. Reflection *in* Action involves noticing feelings, thought patterns, and behavioral responses as they happen, choosing how to respond moment by moment. It's reflecting on an experience as it occurs, requiring us to assess the situation, consider how to act, and then act immediately. Nurses are experts in this type of reflective practice. For instance, you're caring for an elderly patient, and on your initial assessment, you notice that the call bell is out of her reach. Knowing your patient is a high risk for falls, you immediately move the call bell where she can reach it, ensuring that all of the high-risk fall protocols are in place. While Reflection *in* Action is important and valuable because it can produce immediate and effective solutions in real time, this reflection process may end with the event itself, and personal learning may not occur to the same degree. Reflective practice involves recapturing the experience, then analyzing and evaluating it in an effort to gain new knowledge. When a person can rethink and retell their experiences, it is easier to organize and categorize the emotions and ideas surrounding the event and then to compare the intended purpose of the action with the actual results. This describes the third stage reflective practice, which is referred to as **Reflection *for* Action**. This is the stage in which we combine the lessons learned with the intention to apply knowledge in professional and personal lives. The ability to step back from an experience permits critical reflection on the sequence of events (Paterson et al., 2013).

An Example of "Reflection *on* Action" in Jane's World

Jane, a new charge nurse, presents the patient assignments to her team prior to the beginning of her shift. Rhonda, one of the more senior nurses, pulls Jane aside and complains about her assignment, saying that it is unfair. Jane becomes flustered and angry with Rhonda's comments. She angrily tells Rhonda that if she doesn't like the assignment, then she needs to make it herself. She gives the assignment sheet to Rhonda and storms away from the huddle.

1. **Re-Inhabit:** Later that day, Jane revisits the experience she had with Rhonda.
2. **Reflect**: She acknowledges that she lost her temper unnecessarily and acted unprofessionally.
3. **Review**: Jane reflects on the experience and critically analyzes the moment. She realizes that she feels insecure in the role of charge nurse and doesn't feel comfortable with some of her decisions. She also acknowledges that she became defensive in response to Rhonda's comment and acted out of frustration and fear.
4. **Reframe**: Jane admits she may need some additional training in the role of charge nurse. She also knows that Rhonda is an experienced and highly respected nurse who has supported her in the past. In reflecting on the experience, she develops an action plan—*reflection for action*. She schedules a meeting with her manager to discuss tools available that will assist her in becoming a more confident and skilled charge nurse. She also decides to meet with Rhonda one on one to discuss the experience in order to rebuild the relationship and to gain understanding of and perspective into Rhonda's comments. Jane knows this lesson will enable her to become a better charge nurse.

Reflective Practice: Your Superpower

There are many models that can be used as a framework in establishing a meaningful and effective reflective practice. All focus on the basic stages of reflection, understanding, and action. We'll cover two models: one designed to manage coaching and team debriefs, The Gibbs Reflective Cycle, and the second designed as an individual-level model for reflective journaling, *Shifts*. The Gibbs Reflective Cycle, a model developed by Graham Gibbs in 1988, is a well- known model for reflective learning, both for individuals and groups or teams. The model is designed as a cyclical process, focusing on five elements. Each element encourages the use of critical reflection, empathy, and individual ownership. The elements include: **Description, Feelings, Evaluation, Analysis,** and **Conclusion/ Action Plan.** Within the framework of the model, each element requires you to think about and work through specific questions in order to develop insights about how you would do things differently, what skills you need to develop, and who and what could support you in your development and growth. There needs to be a balance of subjective and objective thought surrounding the experience. Objective thought is based on facts and observations and is provable, unbiased, and true. Subjective thought is based on assumptions, beliefs, and opinions. These thoughts can be biased and reflect our personal outlook.

Coaching Using the Gibbs Reflection Model: Jane's Story

Let's revisit Jane's experience. She decides to set up a meeting with her mentor, Paula, to discuss the experience and to gain insight into any lessons learned. Paula decides to reflect on the experience with Jane using the Gibbs Reflective model, which is a cyclical model and an effective tool to use in a coaching relationship. She asks Jane to describe what happened, when it happened, who was there, and what was the end result **(Description)**. Next, Paula encourages Jane to talk about her thoughts and feelings related to the experience **(Feelings)**. She uses questions: What did you feel before this incident? What did you feel after this incident? How do you feel now? She also asks Jane to reflect on the feelings of the other people involved. Paula understands that talking about feelings may be difficult, so she uses empathetic listening to help her see and feel the experience from Jane's point of view. Paula now knows that Jane needs to look objectively at the approaches she used that did and didn't work **(Evaluation)**. She asks Jane to reflect on both the positives and negatives of the experience and asks her to identify those things that went well and those things that didn't go well. Paula steers Jane in analyzing the experience in an effort to determine the root cause of the issue and then helps Jane draw conclusions as to why the incident occurred **(Analysis)**. Paula encourages Jane to think about the situation again, using the information collected. She then asks Jane the following questions **(Conclusions/ Action Plan):** How could this have been a more positive experience for everyone involved? If the situation were to happen again, what would you do differently? And finally, what skills need to be developed to support growth and development? Paula works with Jane to develop and commit to an action plan and schedules a follow-up meeting.

Figure 11

Gibbs Reflective Cycle

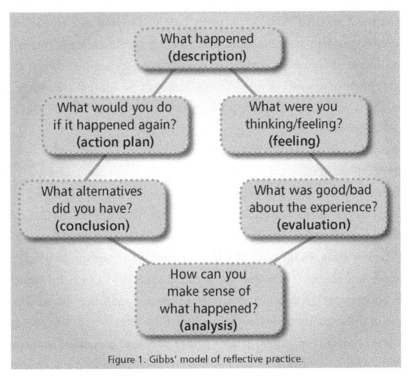

Figure 1. Gibbs' model of reflective practice.

Note: From Gibbs, G. (1988). *Learn by doing: A guide to teaching and learning methods.* Farther Education Unit.

Reflective practice in healthcare is viewed as an important strategy for learning and is seen as an effective methodology to use in an environment that is complex and constantly changing. Researcher Adrienne Price (2004) argues that embracing a reflective practice helps nurses to further understand motives, perceptions, attitudes, values, and feelings associated with patient care; to provide a new outlook on situations that can arise in practice; to challenge existing thoughts, feelings, and actions; and to discover different ways to approach situations.

Developing and adhering to a reflective practice that aides in self-development requires personal commitment and dedication. However, there can be barriers. Lack of time has been cited as one reason people lose interest in establishing a structured reflective practice. Let's go back to my first diary. When I started journaling, I made a practice of writing in my diary every night before I went to sleep. Over time, I trained myself to become focused and intentional with my reflection, and soon, it became a habit. Having the time to reflect should be a part of your daily self-care regimen. Even if your reflective practice consists of just a few minutes, a few minutes on regular basis can be effective in supporting the pause necessary to rethink and reevaluate an experience or event.

Distractions can also be a barrier. Try not to allow yourself to be distracted by interruptions during your reflective time. Turn off your phone, TV, or whatever else may steal your attention. Find a space that is quiet and safe. A successful reflective practice requires your full attention and should incorporate the self-care habits of mindfulness and self-compassion while addressing your experiences without judgement or self-criticism. There needs to be a balance of subjective and objective thought about the experience. Purposeful breathing, which encourages the brain waves responsible for reducing distraction and increasing the capacity to focus, is a wonderfully effective tool to use as you begin your reflective practice. It also brings you into a state of mindfulness and calm, which, in turn, helps support the processes of reflection, objectivity, and learning.

Within the professional world, not every organization is open to the concept of reflective practice, and the lack of support from leaders may hinder the process. In nursing, however, reflective practice is seen as a core component for professional growth and as a potential antidote for nurse burnout and compassion fatigue. Self-reflection helps reconnect to purpose by helping reaffirm why we do what we do.

As Upholders, we understand that one of the greatest challenges we face as complex humans is knowing who we are and what matters to us. Giving ourselves the time and space to reflect on our experiences and embracing our humanity is the "superpower" needed to meet that challenge.

Reflective Journaling: The New Diary

The benefits of having a reflective practice are many, but most importantly, it provides us with the ability to help restore a sense of personal well-being and purpose. Reflection is our "pause" from doing to being, from action to thought. Reflective practice promotes self-compassion, gratitude, and brings personal insight and connection to self and to others. When used as a professional growth and development tool, it provides insight and helps identify how effective or ineffective our actions and decisions are. Reflective practice allows you to see things from someone else's perspective, not just your own, and can help shed light on situations, revealing alternative ways to solve issues that you might have missed had you not taken the time to pause. But why journal?

Reflective journaling helps us make sense of events and experiences that have occurred in our lives. It allows us to speculate on why things are the way they are. Journaling allows us to decompress by getting thoughts out of our head. When we write experiences down, including feelings and actions associated with the experience, we are better able to see whether our experience aligned with our values, or if, in the future, we need to adjust our actions to better align with our values. We all have the capacity to grow, to learn new skills, and to prepare ourselves for future opportunities. The act of reflective journaling allows us to document our interpretations of our experience and the lessons learned from that experience. When we can relate a learning opportunity to our actual experience, we develop a deeper understanding of that experience. The journal becomes our tool.

Journaling is not a new concept. It has been around for hundreds of years. The act of writing down thoughts, feelings, and ideas is a form of self-expression that can lead to increased self-awareness and personal growth. Journaling is a skill, and just like with any skill, the more you practice the better you become. However, getting started can sometimes be a challenge.

Practicing reflective journaling is sometimes easier when there is a framework to guide our reflection. Remember the Gibbs model for reflective practice? While that model is sound and particularly effective when used for debriefing teams or for one-on-one coaching, what if there was a journaling framework for nurses designed to mirror how nurses think, communicate, and process information?

Shifts is a journal designed by nurses, for nurses. As the title implies, the practice of reflective thinking and reflective journaling will often cause a *shift* in the way we perceive experiences and life events. Reflective practice provides us the opportunity to shift our perspective, our attitude, and our behavior, creating a positive shift in our personal growth.

The journal uses an SBAR format, a familiar and standardized communication tool used in healthcare, and steers you to reflect first on your own health and well-being. As a Human-Centered Leader, you understand and support the concept that "it starts with you," and this is exactly where your reflective practice should begin. The journaling process asks you to identify and commit to an intention. The intention is used to help manifest the personal and professional goals and vision you have for yourself. The intention can be general or specific, but it needs to be positive in tone and flexible. The journaling process will challenge you to reflect on how your experiences influence your intention. When you place your well-being at the center, as a lens to reflect on experiences, situations, or events, you just might discover the need to shift your original intention.

Shifts: For more information on *Shifts*, the nursing journal created for nurses by nurses, please visit www.uleadership.com.

The SBAR format for reflective journaling begins with **Situation**. Reflect on an experience or event, big or small, positive or negative, that impacted your day. What happened? When did it happen? Where did it happen? Were other people involved? After describing the experience/situation in as much detail as you feel necessary, move your thoughts to the next step, **Background.** Here, you're encouraged to focus on how your sense of well-being influenced the experience or situation. For example, as you focus on self-care, or the physical aspects of well-being, ask yourself questions like: Am I eating foods that are healthy and clean? Am I drinking plenty of fluids to keep me hydrated? Am I getting enough quality sleep? Am I exercising my body? As you begin to reflect on your mental health, ask yourself these questions: Do I take time out of each day to pause, breathe, and be present in the moment? Am I finding the time to nurture my relationships with friends and family? Self-compassion is an important facet of reflective journaling, so think about the following questions: Am I experiencing negative self-talk during my day? Did I expect perfection from myself today? What am I doing to stay mentally healthy? Did I do something over the past 24 hours that brought me joy? Finally, how self-aware did you feel today? What stressed you out? What made you happy or angry? How did your emotions impact you? How did your emotions impact others? Self-care means many things to many people, but in simple terms, it means you taking care of you. We all know we respond to situations based on how we feel physically, mentally, emotionally, and spiritually. It's okay to acknowledge that we might, at times, fail at self-care. It happens to the best of us. Reflective journaling should provide you with the acumen to see where those gaps in your self-care practice may lie.

In the **Assessment** stage, you are encouraged to use your thoughts and insights to analyze and evaluate your experience. Ask yourself questions such as: What is really going on? What am I learning about myself? How does what I'm learning about myself align with my intention? Answering these questions in an honest and authentic way encourages an openness and vulnerability within yourself. The **Recommendation** portion challenges you to reflect on areas you identify as strengths, as well as opportunities for growth. Developing a plan of action to address the opportunities you've identified becomes the foundation for growth and development. Ask yourself the following questions: What would I do differently if this situation were to ever happen again? Where did I shine? Where is my opportunity? You may even take this as an opportunity to question whether you need to make changes to your original intention. Let's look at an example of reflective journaling using the SBAR framework with Jane's experience.

Example of a Journal Entry Using Jane's Story

My 30-day Intention: To give myself grace

S (Situation): I didn't sleep well last night knowing that I had "charge" duty today, and I ended up sleeping through my alarm. I got to work and quickly made the assignment. After huddle, Rhonda pulled me aside and told me that she didn't think her assignment was fair, which really made me angry and frustrated. I told Rhonda to "deal with it" and that I didn't appreciate her questioning my decision. The shift was crazy. I ran around all day putting out fires, and I didn't get to eat anything until mid-afternoon. I kept thinking about my interaction with Rhonda, and I avoided her all day.

B (Background): I know I stayed up too late last night watching a movie, and when I finally got to bed, I had a hard time going to sleep. I was worried about being in charge. I didn't eat or drink like I should have, which made me even more nervous and tense. I'm also really mad at myself for losing my temper with Rhonda.

A (Assessment): This day started out wrong. I overslept and then raced to work, already stressed out about being in charge. When Rhonda pulled me aside and told me she thought her assignment was unfair, I was embarrassed and defensive. I just recently started taking on the charge nurse role, and I don't feel comfortable with some of my decisions. I think some of the more senior nurses are always judging me because I'm new to this role. Sometimes I don't feel supported by the team. I really like Rhonda and have a lot of respect for her. It hurt my feelings that she challenged my decision. In retrospect, Rhonda's assignment was unfair. I gave her two difficult patients without tech support. I made a mistake in my decision. My intention is to give myself grace, and to forgive myself for my mistakes, my lapse in judgement and my hurtful behavior. I know I have more to learn with regards to being a charge nurse. Even though I made a mistake with Rhonda's assignment, I'm proud I was able to support my team by effectively handling some immediate issues that were affecting their workflow. I know I don't know all of the "tricks of the trade" yet, but I'll keep moving forward.

R (Recommendation): First of all, I need to make sure I take better care of myself by getting to bed at a decent hour. I also need to schedule some time with my manager to see if she knows of a charge nurse class I can take. I need to meet with Rhonda to apologize for my outburst. I'm also going to see if Paula, my mentor, can meet me for lunch tomorrow. I would love to get her advice. Tomorrow is a new day!!

Human-Centered Leadership and Reflective Practice

Reflective learning is a practice involving the identification and exploration of different perspectives, both subjective and objective, in order to deepen the learning experience. The Human-Centered Leader, as an Upholder, understands the concept that "it starts with me, but it's not about me." By maintaining a strong sense of *personal well-being*, as well as embracing an *others-oriented* mindset, the Upholder, through reflective practice, champions growth and seeks to reveal within others what they themselves may not be able to see (Leclerc et.al., 2020). The Human-Centered Leader, as an Awakener, serves in the role as *coach* and *mentor*, and through reflective practice, they stress critical thinking, provide honest feedback, and expect accountability for individual growth plans (Leclerc et.al., 2020). Reflective practice within the concept of Human-Centered Leadership fosters, supports, and encourages life-long learning.

DISCUSSION QUESTIONS

1. What implications might a strong reflective practice have on both your professional and personal life?
2. Think about your own journaling experience. What are some common barriers you encountered? What made it easier for you to journal effectively and routinely?
3. Discuss how you can integrate reflective practice into your team huddles, meetings, or 1:1s.

4. If you could wave a magic wand and give yourself the insights, knowledge, and skills you need in order to succeed this week, what would you give yourself and why?

REFLECTION

Think of an experience or situation, either personally or professionally, where the outcome may not have been what you expected. Go through the Gibbs model of reflective practice. What lessons did you learn? How might you do things differently?

____

____

____

____

____

____

REFERENCES

Gibbs, G. (1988). *Learn by doing: A guide to teaching and learning methods.* Farther Education Unit.

Lawrence-Wilkes, L. (2015). *Reflective practice.* Business Balls. www.businessballs.com/self-awareness/reflective practice

Leclerc, L., Kennedy, K., & Campis, S. (2020). Human-centered leadership in healthcare: An idea that's time has come. *Nursing Administration Quarterly,* 44(2), 117–126.

Paterson, C., & Chapman, J. (2013, August). Enhancing skills of critical reflection to evidence learning in professional practice. *Physical Therapy in Sport,* 14(3), 133–138. https://doi.org/10.1016/j.ptsp2013.03.004

Price, A. (2004, August). Encouraging reflection and critical thinking in practice. Nursing Standard, 18(47), 46–52.

Vague, N. (2019, June 4). *Reflective practice: A leadership superpower*. Evolving Leaders. https://www.evolvingleaders.com.au/reflective-practice-a-leadership-super-power/

Smith, M. K. (2011). Donald Schon: learning, reflection and change. The Encyclopedia of Pedagogy and Informed Education. https://infed.org/mobi/donald-schon-learning (Originally published in 2001).

RECOMMENDED READING

Chartered Institute of Personnel and Development. (2020). *Core behaviours: Lesson 5: Reflect on experience*. The People Profession. https://peopleprofession.cipd.org/learning/learning-passion/reflection

Pellicer, L. O. (2008). *Caring enough to lead: How reflective practice leads to moral leadership* (3rd ed.). Corwin Press.

Chapter 14

Innovation—The Power of Thinking Differently

"Vulnerability is the birthplace of innovation, creativity and change."
—**Brené Brown** (2013), American Storyteller, Researcher, and Author

The Human-Centered Leader recognizes that all leadership is local and that decisions should be designed and implemented by those whose work environment are impacted. The leader must ensure that processes, policies, and resources are in place to allow for and support the development of innovation.

Aesop's Wisdom: The Crow and the Pitcher

A crow perishing with thirst saw a pitcher, and hoping to find water, flew to it with delight. When he reached it, he discovered to his grief that it contained so little water that he could not possibly get at it. He tried everything he could think of to reach the water, but all his efforts were in vain. At last, he collected as many stones as he could carry and dropped them one by one with his beak into the pitcher until he brought the water within his reach and thus saved his life. The moral: Necessity is the mother of invention.

Not only did the crow save his own life, he also learned to think about the world differently. He learned to use tools to help him solve problems. Now that he understood that he was capable of interacting with the world in a different way, through the use of tools and objects, his paradigm changed—he thought differently. More possibilities were open to him. He had new ways of solving problems.

Human-Centered Leadership and Innovation

Have you ever worked in a hospital that expected market-leading results but didn't want to change anything? Or maybe the only suitable changes were those that came from the top of the organization? With traditional leadership, this is often the case. It's easier to stick with the status quo than to risk making an error that might not be well received. But what about organizations that take a more contemporary, human-centered approach, and value risk-taking? How do their leaders practice differently? How do the bedside caregivers think differently? In this chapter, we'll explore innovation from the perspective of the Human-Centered Leader. We'll discuss innovative competencies for leaders and bedside nurses and look at ways to teach innovation in academia and practice.

The Human-Centered leader engages the attributes of the Awakener, the Connector, and the Upholder to create an environment where individuals work together to develop innovative solutions. The Awakener, who focuses on continuous learning, encourages risk-taking when the team is working towards a solution. The Awakener values mistakes because they contribute rich learning. Thomas Edison once explained, "I have not failed. I've just found 10,000 ways that won't work." A culture of excellence, cultivated by the Awakener, coexists with innovation to ultimately provide market-leading outcomes.

The Connector collaborates with their team and across the organization to bring interdisciplinary professionals together for innovative problem-solving. This requires an organizational culture that embraces innovation throughout all levels of leadership and at the point of care. Ensuring an innovative culture in the organization is the most critical competency for leaders if they are to promote risk-taking and innovation. The culture of trust, created by the Connector, frees team members to think outside the box, knowing the organizational structures are there to support them.

The Upholder, who focuses on relationships and humanness, nurtures engagement within the team and helps them see meaning and purpose in their work. Each team member is highly valued for their strengths and their ability to contribute to creative problem-solving. The caring environment provides fertile ground for innovation to take root.

Human-Centered Leaders are mindful. If a decision is not urgent, requiring an immediate solution, they consider various perspectives and use abductive reasoning to ask, "What if?" They focus on the desired new state and then explore ways to get there. Many possibilities and opportunities exist—the goal is to find "a better way." This requires a paradigm shift from the "risk-adverse" mindset to one of "embracing risk in search of a better way."

Walking the Talk

Cleveland Clinic provides a great example of an organization that embraces risk-taking, creativity, and innovation. On Cleveland Clinic's blog, *Consult QD*, Kelly Hancock, DNP, RN, NE-BC, FAAN (2018), Chief Caregiver Officer and past Executive Chief Nursing Officer, explains that innovative thinking is considered a professional responsibility for nurses at all levels of the organization. In their program, *Innovation Inventory*, nurses are acknowledged for implementing innovative processes or systems as part of their usual work to meet desired outcomes. This inventory list of point-of-care innovations employed by staff nurses is highly valued and tracked by the organization. In addition, Cleveland Clinic has two other innovation programs designed to engage nursing in bigger thinking, outside the usual work on their unit. The *I Innovate* program allows nurses to submit new ideas for change or improvement within the organization. Their submissions are reviewed and considered for further development. Idea generation is a part of their annual employee appraisal process and is integrated into the professional ladder program. Lastly, a third program, *Step Forward*, helps nurses develop their ideas into solutions. They're paired with an innovation coordinator, and their work is processed through the Cleveland Clinic Innovations team. As you can see, the leaders and the structures of the organization support and encourage innovation at the point of care (Hancock, 2018).

Awaken Bedside Nurses to Shift their Paradigm

Since a paradigm shift results in thinking differently, what ideas can the Awakener use to coach and challenge the nursing team to develop innovative thinking? What changes in thinking will bring about mindful observations and creativity? Horth and Buchner (2014) suggest the following ways to promote creative thinking: **pay close attention** to routine tasks; **personalize the work** by considering your experiences or your patient's experiences; **use imagination** to envision the possibilities and ask "What if?"; engage in **serious play** to have fun and be less critical of ideas; use **collaborative inquiry** with colleagues; and lastly, use **crafting** to make intuitive connections between seemingly unrelated concepts. The story below illustrates how a nursing team used these techniques to promote innovative thinking and create an improvement in practice.

Thinking Differently

A burn program in a large public hospital treated both adult and pediatric patients from across their state. One group of nurses was particularly interested in the care of pediatric patients. They formed a subgroup within the NPG council to consider innovative ways to enhance the care provided to these children. Ethel, one of the nurses on the team, had noticed that her pediatric patients sometimes seemed bored and even depressed (**pay close attention**). She thought they'd benefit from distractions to help them cope with their injuries and care procedures. During one of the team's council meetings, Ethel shared her observations with her colleagues and asked, "What changes could we make to bring joy and normalcy to these children's lives, so they are better able to cope and heal?" (**collaborative inquiry**). Ethel personalized the problem and shared with the team that one of her patients, Joshua, didn't have family to visit. He needed more interaction with others and distraction from his daily care. Ethel also talked about how her own children liked playing games and doing simple crafts (**personalizing the problem**). The team began to imagine all the possibilities. Could they develop a playroom and a playtime program? The ideas started flowing…

"Why don't we bring in a play station and some video games?"

"We definitely need nurses' and doctors' kits for imaginary play along with building blocks to develop their motor skills."

"I wonder if we could find a clown to visit routinely?" (**engage in serious play**).

They began connecting many different ideas: the physical environment, a play therapist, the Hospital Foundation for fund raising, and a local fire department for additional donations and support (**crafting to make intuitive connections**). Because their organization valued innovative thinking, and their leader was 100% behind them in this effort, an office space was soon renovated to create a children's playroom. The design was based on best practices the nurses learned from reviewing the literature, visiting pediatric hospitals, and consulting with both play therapists and architects. A full-time play therapist was hired, and an entire play program was developed. This innovation and enhancement in care was directly attributed to the nurses, who wanted to improve the care provided to their patients. Consider the impact this project had on the nurses who saw their innovation come to fruition. Think about the difference this innovation had on the lives of their pediatric patients and families. Imagine Ethel and the other nurses on the team thinking to themselves, "This is why I became a nurse."

When is Innovation Needed? Mind the Gap

Nurses have historically been innovative. They do whatever is necessary to take care of their patients. If you think back to Florence Nightingale, you'll remember her innovations around improving the physical environment of the injured and sick soldiers during the Crimean War. She recorded her data to demonstrate the value of her innovation, and this forever changed the way healthcare workers think about the environment's impact on healing. With COVID-19, we saw nurses consistently innovating to improve care to their patients. They developed ways to decrease the use of their short supply of PPE (personal protective equipment) by bundling care at the patient's bedside, extending tubing on IV pumps so they could be adjusted outside the patient's room, and writing on the windows of the

ICU room to communicate the need for additional supplies. They used different models of care based on available resources, such as redeployment of nurses to high volume areas and team nursing in critical care units. They even taught people in the community how to sew masks. They saw the need for innovation and filled the gap with creative solutions.

Porter-O'Grady and Malloch (2018) ask the question, "*When* should we innovate in practice?" When is what we already know not enough anymore? They recommend looking at the following three areas to identify gaps: knowledge creation and research, clinical expertise, and patient values. Is there is a gap in current knowledge and practice? Is there a gap in clinical expertise? Is there is a difference between what the patient values and current practice? These gaps point to the need for innovative solutions in the form of enhancement, advancement, or creativity. The NPG council provides a structure for the team to think differently and come up with creative ideas to close the gaps.

Opportunities for Innovation:

1. **Gap in knowledge or research**—Examples of successful initiatives reported by the American Academy of Nursing include programs to promote and protect breast-feeding in vulnerable infants, assist the elderly in remaining in their homes, improve caregiver skills, provide affordable and culturally sensitive community and family healthcare services, and strengthen parenting skills (AAN, 2020).

2. **Gap in clinical expertise** -Examples of nurse innovations to improve clinical practice include: the crash cart; neonatal phototherapy; ColorSafe IV Lines for easy identification of lines; Neo-slip to help patients put on compression hose; and a feeding tube for paralyzed veterans (Guyton, 2018).

3. **Gap in patient values**—Examples of nurse innovations around patients' values include: infant wear tailored with an opening for parents to provide umbilical cord care; a caregiver connections program to connect care seekers with potential caregivers; collaborative care clinics for

population health, e.g. Alzheimer's; hospital innovation units focused on patient-centered care; and mobile discharge instructions that provide a digital recording of the nurse's instructions to improve communication (Wood, 2013).

The Strategic Must-Haves for Innovation

The Human-Centered Leader flourishes in the work environment that values innovation. Porter-O'Grady and Malloch (2018) point to five "must-haves" required to create this supportive environment. Remember the Cleveland Clinic? Let's look at how they exemplify these must-haves. They are:

1. **Integration of innovative thinking into the organizational mission, vision, and values**

   This formally defines the commitment of the organization to innovation and provides the cornerstone supporting innovative structures and processes.

   Example: Cleveland Clinic's mission statement is "To provide better care of the sick, investigation in their problems and further education of those who serve." One of their six values is innovation: "We drive small and large changes to transform healthcare everywhere." One of the strategic goals at the Cleveland Clinic is to "engage caregivers as members of teams."

2. **Assessment of the community and team needs**

   Innovative problem-solving should reflect the needs of the team or the community, otherwise the solutions don't add significant value.

   Example: You can find the annual community health needs assessment online for each hospital within the Cleveland Clinic Organization. In 2019, one of the significant chronic diseases in the community surrounding the main campus was diabetes. The impact of their actions from the previous year are listed in the Highlighted Impact report: "Patients were seen in the outpatient Chronic Disease center. Diabetes education programs—such as healthy cooking classes, nutrition education, support groups and a farmer's market—were provided in East Cleveland, an area with a high incidence of diabetes" (Cleveland Clinic, 2020b; Cleveland Clinic, 2020c).

3. **Supportive organizational structures**

Organizational structures required to support innovation include leadership, reporting structures, decision-making expectations, and systems to document and measure results. These structures reflect the mission, vision, and values which innovative leaders then operationalize with their teams on their unit and department.

Example: Cleveland Clinic employs a model of nursing shared governance to serve as the formal infrastructure to promote innovation and involve nurses who provide bedside care in shared leadership. Values include collaboration and exchange of ideas; continuous learning, decision-making, innovative, and participatory change management, and engaged action regarding practice and the practice environment (Cleveland Clinic, 2020d).

4. **Supportive innovation processes**

There's a natural tension for leaders supporting innovation processes. They must balance the safety and stability of operations with the need to explore innovations for continuous improvement. Other supportive processes are also needed: incorporating innovative thinking as a core competency; embracing "thinking differently" among diverse teams; providing time for reflection and idea generation; recognizing and rewarding innovative thinking; and incorporating multiple levels of collaboration and teamwork in the innovative process.

Example: The Cleveland Clinic supports the innovation process through multiple programs: *Innovation Inventory, I Innovate*, and *Step Forward*. Innovations move from the *Step Forward* program to the *Cleveland Clinic Innovations* organization. This is a commercialization arm that turns breakthrough innovations from caregivers into medical products and companies that benefit patients (Hancock, 2018).

5. **Measuring results**

As innovations are implemented, the intended (and possibly, unintended) results must be monitored and measured over time to determine the value of the innovation in improving patient safety and quality care.

Example: At the Cleveland Clinic the *Innovation Inventory* tracks innovative changes and solutions implemented at the unit level. These are changes that have been implemented, monitored, and measured over time. Idea generation is tracked in annual employee appraisals, and projects around innovation are included in the professional ladder program (Hancock, 2018).

When assessing an organization for professional fit and further growth, a Human-Centered Leader does well to consider whether these must-haves are in place or whether the organization is on the road to acknowledging the importance of innovation in meeting the undeniable changes and challenges of today's healthcare environment.

Innovation Competencies

So, what are the competencies that leaders need to be innovative? White et. al. (2016) developed a list of 19 competencies to promote leadership innovation. They surveyed over 1400 nurse leaders who rated the importance of each skill and their level of competence in each skill. Of the 19 skills, only one—tenacity and perseverance—rated high in both importance and level of competency. In other words, leaders felt the skills were important, but they didn't feel completely competent to perform them. The five skills recognized as the **most important for nurse leaders supporting innovation** are listed in Table 14 along with the Human-Centered Leadership dimensions that support each of the competencies.

Table 14

Crosswalk of Innovation Competencies with Human-Centered Leadership

Innovation Competencies	Brief Definition of Competency	Human-Centered Leader Dimension
1. Ability to convey a compelling vision	Capable of conveying a vision of the innovation and its potential impact in ways that are compelling.	Connector
2. Resilience	Tendency of an individual to cope with stressful, adverse, and devastating situations; to be able to recover from failures; and to constructively sustain efforts of pursuing goals.	Upholder
3. Ability to recognize an opportunity	Scan and search for new information, "connect the dots" between incidents that appear to be unrelated with limited cues and recognize patterns or ideas that suggest potential opportunities in the myriad cues or signals that they receive.	Awakener
4. Tenacity and perseverance	Commitment to seeing their vision through, able to endure the long journey to implement innovation, able to work fervently despite challenges or adversity, able to maintain interests, and persist in efforts to achieve goals.	Upholder
5. Interdisciplinary teamwork and collaboration	Ability to communicate and work with members of different professions and disciplines; appreciate and understand different professional cultures; and understand equality in responsibilities and reciprocity.	Connector

Note: Adapted from White, K. R., Pillay, R., & Huang, X. (2016). Nurse leaders and the innovation competence gap. *Nursing Outlook*, 64, 255-261.

The Human-Centered Leadership model provides an easy and practical framework for a leader who is prepared to lead innovation. The Awakener is focused on cultivating people, which means they are always looking for opportunities. These opportunities generally revolve around personnel development and improving excellence. The Connector conveys a compelling vision and unites the team around that vision. The Connector also collaborates with the team and across the organization to support interdisciplinary problem-solving and innovative thinking. Remember the Connector brings unity to the community! The Upholder models self-care and resiliency, which enables perseverance and tenacity. By embracing the attributes of the outward-focused Human-Centered Leader, your leadership behaviors will lead to innovative thinking among your team members.

Teaching Innovation

The most preferred method for teaching innovation is through nonlinear case studies. Students can learn from case studies that demonstrate both success and failure (White et. al. 2016). We don't often think about using examples of failures as a teaching method, but as we know from experience, we learn more from failures than from successes. Bill Gates once said, "Success is a lousy teacher. It makes you think that you can't lose." IBM's Thomas J. Watson, Sr., wisely advised, "If you want to succeed, double your failure rate." These ideas certainly go against our human nature and our fear of failure. This is why the Human-Centered Leader's courage to show vulnerability and authenticity is key to modeling innovative thinking.

Consider the teaching methods discussed in Chapter 12 on capability. These same nonlinear methods are helpful when teaching innovation: small problem-solving groups, case studies, stories, and simulation. As you probably guessed, traditional lectures are the least relevant in teaching innovation (White et. al., 2016). Nonlinear teaching methods may be incorporated into both formal education in academia and continuing education in practice. Uniting clinical and academic leaders helps to promote innovative competencies. Clinical leaders bring real workplace experiences into the classroom. In return academic leaders, collaborating in the practice setting, help nursing teams identify gaps, look for opportunities for innovative thinking, and promote discovery.

Learning from Failure

A patient experience leader in a large community hospital wanted to "inspire" the nursing staff to elevate and celebrate caring moments with their patients. He suggested that the nurses write up their experiences and the NPG council celebrate some of these nurses by transferring their pictures to "skins" that would cover the elevator doors. The idea was to promote the care exhibited by the nursing staff to both internal and external customers. Unfortunately, upper leadership was not on board with this idea and felt it would negatively impact the professional appearance of the hospital. The nurses were very disappointed since they had already moved forward with writing and reviewing nurses' experiences. The **key learning** from this failed idea was that simply "thinking outside the box" is insufficient in establishing innovation. To support innovative thinking and decisions, the structures and processes must be clear and integrated throughout the organization.

Nurse Innovators

Thanks to social media and the development of on-line communities, there are now more opportunities for nurse innovators to join other healthcare providers and leaders outside healthcare to develop solutions to problems around patient care. MakerNurse, a collaborative effort supported by MIT and the Robert Wood Johnson Foundation, is an online community that supports the ingenuity of nurses who innovate at the bedside. In addition, Nurse Hackathons have gained popularity by bringing together large, diverse groups of individuals who work together over an entire weekend to propose solutions to significant problems. The 2020 Hackathon, sponsored by Johnson & Johnson, brought together nurses, other healthcare professionals, and Microsoft engineers to develop technological solutions for COVID-19 challenges. Johnson & Johnson further invests in nurses through their two-year fellowship for nurse innovators. They accept nurse innovators with strong leadership and entrepreneurial potential into the fellowship and develop them further as an investment in the future of healthcare transformation.

Ignite Innovation

Nurse leaders, who embrace the attributes of the Human-Centered Leader, *Awaken* their teams to innovation through mentoring, coaching, and providing the structure for innovation to take place. They ensure the environment promotes continuous learning and that the team feels free to take risks. The *Connector*, who models edgewalking, invites others to join them on the edge by providing support, advocacy, and collaborative problem-solving. The *Upholder* believes in the team and in their ability to creatively solve problems around the gaps in clinical knowledge, practice, and values. The Upholder navigates the social and organizational environment to ensure that risk-taking is supported with processes, policies, and resources. The Human-Centered Leader naturally supports innovative thinking by embracing risk-taking, learning from mistakes, and working collaboratively with their team and across the organization. Through leading in a different, outward-focused manner, the Human-Centered Leader's behaviors promote a positive culture. This culture offers an empowering environment for nurses to lead the way in transforming the future of healthcare. Innovation is ignited!

DISCUSSION QUESTIONS

1. When you think of the word "innovation" what comes immediately to your mind? Positive words and ideas? If so, share. Negative words and ideas? If so, share.
2. How can you, as a Human-Centered Leader, encourage or incentivize innovation among your team?
3. Think about the work of your team over the last year or so. What innovative ideas have been developed during the nurses' usual bedside care? What bigger ideas impacting teams beyond your unit have been developed?

REFLECTION

Having an innovation-based mission ensures support for innovative thinking. Think about your particular unit or department or college. If you could dream big, what would your mission statement be?

_____

_____

_____

_____

_____

_____

REFERENCES

American Academy of Nursing. (n.d.) *Edge runner profiles*. Retrieved December 13, 2020 from https://www.aannet.org/initiatives/edge-runners/profiles

Brown, B. (2013, May 11). *Can We Gain Strength From Shame?* [Interview]. TED Radio Hour with Guy Raz. https://www.npr.org/2013/08/23/174033560/can-we-gain-strength-from-shame

Cleveland Clinic. (2020a). *Mission, vision, values.* https://my.clevelandclinic.org/about/overview/who-we-are/mission-vision-values

Cleveland Clinic. (2020b). *2019 Cleveland Clinic Health System CHNAs and implementation strategy reports.* https://my.clevelandclinic.org/about/community/reports/community-health-needs-assessment-reports#2019-chnas-tab

Cleveland Clinic (2020c). *Community health needs assessment 2019.* https://my.clevelandclinic.org/-/scassets/files/org/about/community-reports/chna/2019/2019-cleveland-clinic-main-campus-chna.ashx?la=en

Cleveland Clinic. (2020d). *Nursing Institute: Shared governance.* https://my.clevelandclinic.org/departments/nursing/about/shared-governance

Guyton, N. (2018, May 8). *6 healthcare innovations you may not know were created by nurses.* Spōk. https://www.spok.com/blog/6-healthcare-innovations-you-may-not-know-were-created-nurses/

Hancock, K. (2018, April 15). *Cleveland Clinic nurses share innovative practice ideas: Innovation center keeps nurses thinking differently*. Consult QD. https://consultqd.clevelandclinic.org/cleveland-clinic-nurses-share-innovative-practice-ideas/

Horth, D., & Buchner, D. (2014). Innovation leadership: How to use innovation to lead effectively, work collaboratively, and drive results. *Center for Creative Leadership*. https://www.ccl.org/wp-content/uploads/2015/04/InnovationLeadership.pdf

Porter-O'Grady, T., & Malloch, K. (2018). *Quantum leadership: Creating sustainable value in health care* (5th ed.). Jones and Bartlett.

Thomas, T. W., Seifert, P. C., & Joyner, J. C. (2016, September 30). Registered nurses leading innovative changes. *The Online Journal of Issues in Nursing*. https://pubmed.ncbi.nlm.nih.gov/27856917/

White, K. R., Pillay, R., & Huang, X. (2016). Nurse leaders and the innovation competence gap. *Nursing Outlook*, 64, 255–261.

Wood, D. (2013). *Putting innovative ideas to work*. RN.com. https://www.rn.com/nursing-news/rns-putting-innovative-ideas-to-work/

RECOMMENDED READING

Clipper, B., Wang, M. Coyne, P., Baiera, V., Love, R., Nix, D., Nix, W., & Weirich, B. (2019). *The nurse's guide to innovation: Accelerating the journey*. Super Star Press.

Weberg, D. & Davidson, S. (2021). *Leadership for evidence-based innovation in nursing and health professions* (2nd ed.). Jones & Bartlett Learning, LLC.

Chapter 15

Dealing with "Joy Interrupters"

"Joy does not simply happen to us. We have to choose joy and keep choosing it every day."
—**Henri J. M. Nouwen**, Dutch Priest, Professor, Writer, and Theologian

You may be thinking Human-Centered Leadership sounds really good, but you may also recognize that not everyone in our world thinks the same way we do. Not everyone in your unit or your organization is human-centered. In fact, there are probably several traditional or transactional leaders who work alongside or above you. As healthcare professionals, we face challenges such as staffing shortages, incivility, workplace violence, lack of control in the workplace, misaligned policies and regulations, and colleagues who interrupt our joy. Richard Ricciardi, the 33rd president of nursing's international honor society and professional organization, Sigma Theta Tau International, recognizes these challenges. Ricciardi (2019) presented a call to action to "infuse joy" to achieve Sigma's vision of global nursing excellence. His call-to-action highlights three essential elements—the ABCs—that promote joy: Awareness, Balance and purpose, and Co-creation. Our global leaders at Sigma are asking us to start locally. We're asking you to see the issues we cited earlier as surmountable and to seize the opportunity to improve our experiences and work cultures by living the attributes of a Human-Centered Leader. So back to the elephant in the room. What do we do when the "joy interrupters" in our world aren't exactly human-centered? We've given that some thought and done some research. Read on. This chapter is all about those "joy interrupters." There are ways to be true to your Human-Centered self while living and working with others who have different ways of leading. Keep in mind, being part of a revolution takes courage.

One of the most common questions we get is, "What do I do if I'm a Human-Centered Leader but many of those around me are traditional, transactional, or just plain toxic?" Simply put, "What do I do when someone interrupts my joy?" As with any hard question, there's not going to be an easy answer. What we can do, however, is offer tangible and evidence-based actions that will help you maintain your joy. Keep in mind, our mantra is to start with ourselves, so managing "joy interrupters" hinges on how we respond. As with any situation involving human beings, we have choices. We can assess, observe, evaluate the situation, and make a conscious decision on how we choose to react to those joy interrupters. Let's illustrate the actions we can take through tales of two real-world experiences. One tale revolves around a team primarily comprised of Human-Centered Leaders; and the other tells the story of a team with very few Human-Centered Leaders.

Uninterrupted Joy … For the Most Part

When I first entered the executive nursing leadership world, I was lucky to work directly for a chief nursing officer I now recognize as a Human-Centered Leader. Celeste brought me on board with the aim of creating the often-invisible architecture that supports nursing excellence, trust, and caring. Here's the short list of my job description's objectives and roles: create shared governance, develop a clinical ladder program, build a transition to practice/residency program for new graduates, strengthen the clinical educator network, implement research and evidence-based practice programs, cultivate continuing education, facilitate equitable academic-practice partnerships, innovate and transform nurse recruitment and retention, and assist nurses in taking ownership of quality metrics. Pretty daunting, but with the support of a leader who recognized the importance of developing a team of leaders aligned with her approach to Awakening, Connecting, and Upholding, we did all that and more. I was surrounded by other directors who shared the vision for nursing growth and excellence. In the first year, we developed a clinical ladder program to align diverse quality objectives with nurses' passions. Nurses on the front line were awakening to their ability to develop and carry out an evidence-based practice project that improved outcomes. Kelly, an ER nurse, tackled throughput with evidence-based triage, allowing an RN to be at the front desk for intake. Lilly, a hospice nurse, not only met the objectives of the clinical ladder program by implementing an evidence-based classification and documentation system for hospice eligibility, she published her work in the *Journal of Hospice and Palliative Nursing*. The critical care nurses, led by their educator, Robert, developed a nurse-driven research study to evaluate the influence of care bundles in reducing visual, auditory, and sensory stimulation on metrics such as rates of delirium, lengths of stay, number of falls, and instances of patient complications. That team developed the research question, performed the literature review, created the randomization structure, checked inter-rater reliability of the assessment (RAS-CAM), and carried it out with the rigor of a research team. I must point out this was the first nursing research project ever done at this facility. Robert went on to present at a national quality conference, and we collaboratively presented at an international research congress. I still hear from these nurses, their leaders, and Celeste about how the structures we crafted for nursing excellence are sustained to this day. There were few people at that organization who interrupted our joy, but when they did, we learned how to pause, consider the right thing to do, and state our case confidently. When the critical care director was trying to implement open visitation in the ICU, the joy interrupters were her own nurses. You know how it goes when there are a few people who are naysayers who can come up with a million reasons why we shouldn't do something new:

"We can't have family in here all the time. They'll get in the way of all we have to do."

"Families ask so many questions. I like when they're just here for a short while."

"Isn't it against the rules? We can't do this. We've always had limited 10-minute visits."

I could go on and on. The beauty of how Elizabeth, the director, handled it was that she did the following: listened patiently to their concerns; provided evidence to refute their claims; provided evidence to show the positive benefits to the patients, families, and nurses; intentionally allowed the nurses to absorb the evidence; patiently facilitated the process over a period of weeks and months rather than a line in the sand with the start date in two days; and finally, she asked the nurses to consider what was the "right thing to do" for the patients and families. Needless to say, open visitation in the ICU is now the new normal, and the nurses can't imagine going back. Rachel, one of the most resistant ICU RNs said, "I can't believe how helpful most of the families are. I'm noticing the patients responding in different ways. They recognize the voices, the touch."

All the success stories from this organization were possible not only because there was a Human-Centered Leader at the top, but also because the overwhelming spirit of the leadership team was human-centered. Directors, educators, and nurses at the front line had voice in their work environment and were encouraged to walk the edge of change. Celeste enabled edgewalking! Those embedded in the work were handed ownership over themselves, their growth, their environment, and their patients. Celeste built her team with intention. She confidently supported each leader in the spirit of doing what was right for the leader as well as the patients.

Joy, Interrupted

Following such a positive experience in my first director role under Celeste, I moved on to a higher-level executive position at a larger health system. I was hired for a nearly identical role, but many of the programs already existed in different stages of maturation. I thought I had the dream job with a lot less "ground-up" work and more "strengthen the infrastructure" work. I couldn't have been more disillusioned. The biggest challenge was this: while there were a number of directors, nurse managers, and frontline nurses who I would readily identify as Human-Centered Leaders, we were outnumbered by leaders who were transactional, traditional, and downright toxic. Also, at the upper levels of the hospital leadership team, the chief nursing officer was a human-centered leader placed squarely within a legion of highly traditional leaders. Imagine a patchwork of leaders with competing and varying styles, which created an almost palpable tension in huddles, meetings, and day-to-day rounding. The primary focus at the hospital was on metrics like patient satisfaction, hospital acquired infections, and staffing. The pressure on nursing was intense. As in most organizations, nursing had the biggest swath of real estate: patient care, quality metrics, patient satisfaction. Nursing is also almost always the largest workforce in any hospital, and that was true in this hospital. All of these variables aligned to create an interesting and complex architecture requiring a balance between the humans' care, which is our business product, meeting metrics to stay in business, and the ability of leaders to lead those who care for patients. What follows is a unique example of the collision of traditional and human-centered leadership styles.

As a new executive director, I was on my fourth day on the job when one of my team members, a clinical educator, asked me to accompany her to a meeting with the acute care nurse managers and their executive director. The issue at hand was orientation for newly hired RNs and the conflict between unit budgets and budgeted hospital time for orientation. I'll spare you the complicated details, but the nurse managers were aiming to increase the first week's onsite hospital nursing-specific orientation so they could reduce actual time orienting on the unit when the money would hit their budgets and productivity. Not a bad idea, however, the hospital and enterprise-level orientations were squeezing out the ability to do this. Hence, my arrival provided a spark for renewed conversation on the topic. I use the term "conversation" in the most positive light because the actual exchange of dialogue was anything but conversational; rather, it was quite aggressive. Keep in mind this was my fourth day on the job. The executive director, Unma, was known as traditional and proud of her "old school" approach. She mentored her nurse managers in a similar vein. I was assailed with "Well, what are you going to do about it?" to "It's your job to orient our nurses" to "We can't staff our units as it is and have new nurses take up all our money and time." This was my introduction to the acute care leadership team. A few of the nurse managers looked embarrassed and spoke up to pitch in to deliver a "welcome" message near the end of the meeting. In addition to the obvious sense of high-stakes emotions, i.e. anxiety and anger, I did my best to pause in the moment and listen patiently. I thought that possibly, since the role I was filling had been interim for so long, they hadn't really had someone to listen to their concerns. I also forced my best smile and offered that we would provide the best evidence-based effort to support the complex needs of the hospital, the unit-level teams, the department, and the nurses themselves. As I walked away from the meeting and reflected, I developed an intention to dig deeper into the formal and informal leadership structures and relationships within acute care, as well as the other specialty departments. Based on that intention, I mapped out regularly scheduled meetings with each of the specialty department executive directors (critical care, acute care, surgical services, emergency services, and women's services). This allowed us to develop relationships while sharing perspectives on goals, objectives, resources, and innovative ideas for moving our nursing team forward. I discovered rich and fruitful relationships with every department leader. As for Unma, the acute care executive director, our regular meetings certainly helped, but there continued to be instances in which she undermined me and my team. My joy continued to be interrupted. I stayed the course with patience, "evidence-based kindness," intention, and a commitment to doing what was right. In certain situations, when I felt boundaries were crossed, such as micromanaging and criticizing my team members, I would escalate to our shared leader, the Chief Nursing Officer. As stated previously, the CNO was a Human-Centered Leader. It was interesting to watch as Jack, my CNO, addressed our conflict with patience, evidence, kindness, and the intention to do what was right. Following mediation with Jack, Unma and I would ebb and flow in our positive and not-so-positive interactions. Since neither Unma nor I were going anywhere, I learned to expect Unma's "command and control" style and made a cognizant choice to respond with the tools she helped me develop: patience, evidence-based kindness, intention, and aiming to do what was right for my team, for me, for our patients, and for our hospital. In the end, I look back on my experiences with Unma as one of the most valuable learning opportunities of my leadership career. She provided almost daily interactions in which I had to pause and become mindful of the situation at hand. I also became more skilled in my ability to respond in a thoughtful and professional manner and, over time, I realized I had a responsibility to advocate for my own joy and the joy of my team. In the end, I was able to be true to my Human-Centered Leadership style despite consistent challenges. I learned to choose joy every day.

Joy Versus Happiness: Finding joy in our day is different than finding happiness. Joy is generally a result of inner peace and satisfaction. The source of joy lies within us. It's a choice. It's a state of being. In contrast, happiness is generally the result of an external force that brings satisfaction. The source of happiness lies outside of us. It's dependent on external forces. It's temporary. When faced with challenging people or situations, choose joy.

Taking Action: How do I protect my joy?

Patience

In healthcare, there are few conflicts or problems among leaders that are fixed in the moment. Patience requires self-awareness in the situation at hand. Unless there's an immediate threat to life or limb, leaders should pause in the moment to consider the perspectives of each stakeholder. Responding in the heat of the moment to traditional, transactional, or toxic leaders will never fully fix or address the issue. Emotionally intelligent leaders understand and respect the range of human responses that arise during conflict and don't take it personally. If you have a tendency to "take things personally," keep in mind that how others are responding may not have anything to do with you. Remember, through continued practice of mindfulness and self-awareness (external and internal), it's our job as leaders and as humans to become more skilled at how we respond to others (Bradberry & Greaves, 2009). For example, if confronted with an "in-your-face" nurse manager demanding action on staffing challenges, the Human-Centered Leader becomes mindful of the variables surrounding the manager's response and his or her own response. The Human-Centered

Leader may choose to redirect to a time when the manager is calm and prepared to discuss in a professional manner. As Human-Centered Leaders, and just as basic human beings, we should never settle for being talked to in a disrespectful way. Patiently addressing a colleague with facts and a calm demeanor naturally neutralizes some of the emotion. Remember, Robert, the ICU director who wanted to implement open visitation? He recognized the solution to buy-in and success would not appear overnight. He patiently waited for the nurses to find out for themselves the "why" and the benefits. He didn't draw a line in the sand. He did the opposite. He invited the nurses to a wide-open world where they could choose their own path.

Kill Them With Kindness

Many of you have probably seen the slogans on T-shirts and billboards: "Choose Kind." Kindness comes more naturally to some than others. Kindness is free and is clearly a choice. When faced with resistance or conflict, you can't go wrong if you respond with a kind, yet confident and evidence-based reply. According to Patterson et al. (2012), a crucial conversation is one in which there are strong emotions, opposing opinions, and high stakes. The key to successfully navigating a crucial conversation is to have dialogue based in facts. Remove end of the spectrum emotions such as anger and agitation and replace them with evidence and facts. It's hard to argue with evidence, and this tactic will often mitigate the high-stakes emotions of a conflict. The following six basic tactics, suggested by Patterson et al., might help make it more applicable to your world:

1. **Start with the Heart:** This means start the conversation with the right motives. Be clear on what the goal is for you or perhaps for the unit or hospital. Too often, we get caught up in the emotions of the moment and forget the reason we're all in healthcare: caring for our patients and helping them heal. Extend kindness in a way that shows you're invested in the shared vision and goal for quality and safe patient care.

2. **Learn to Look:** Remember when we suggested possibly redirecting or rescheduling a conversation if one or both parties become defensive or

aggressive? That's what we mean by "learn to look." Be mindful about the other person's level of emotion and check your own as well.

3. **Make it Safe:** This folds in the two previous concepts. If you find you or the other party's emotions are escalating, redirect the conversation back to your shared purpose and look for points of agreement. If it's not a safe space for both of you, consider a cooling-off period.

4. **Master your Story:** If you're involved in a situation that makes you personally angry or upset, it's time to call a time-out and take a look at why you feel this way. Dig deep and consider whether previous experiences in life or work are influencing your response. Are you creating a story that's not aligned with the reality of the situation? For example, when we don't have all the details of a situation, we often fill in the gaps with things like, "They're denying additional FTEs for our department because they want to remodel the building." or "They're just shoving this hourly rounding down our throats to improve their numbers." There's always much more to the story than our minds might creatively make up. Before getting angry, ask more questions to clarify.

5. **State your Path and Explore the Path of Others:** This one really hinges on being able to talk in facts and evidence. Take the emotions out of the equation. At the same time, ask the other person for facts that support their view. Perhaps, you can be persuaded to see their point of view in the same way you would like to persuade them. Just the facts, ma'am!

6. **Move to Action:** This is the best tool for nurse leaders who embrace change and innovation. When concluding a crucial conversation or meeting, take a few minutes to come to consensus about the next steps. Build it into every meeting. Build it into every crucial conversation. Document who will do what, by when, and set a date to follow up. We all know "those meetings" where "nothing ever happens." Don't be that leader!

Be Intentional

Intention is a conscious choice to behave in a certain way. It is a mental state in which we evaluate a situation or the day ahead and consider how we aim to meet a goal or objective. For example, many people start their days with an intention to be kind or to drink eight cups of water. It's a powerful tool that can help flip the switch from negative to positive thinking. According to international authors and experts in neuro-linguistic programming (NLP), Tim and Kris Hallbom (2000), intentions trigger your reticular activation system (RAS) which is, simply put, the information filtering system in your brain. An intention sets your focus or brain filter to align with specific goals. As we consider the joy interrupters in our world, intentions become one of the most powerful tools. Human-Centered Leaders use intention as a way to consciously and proactively identify how they will navigate difficult situations and conversations. For example, remember my experience with Unma, the executive director who proudly exercised her traditional, micromanaging leadership style? Part of my journey in learning to live with someone with such a different leadership style was creating intentions for how I would respond to her. Early on, most days were started with an intention to "Pause, be in the moment, relax your facial muscles, and listen to Unma when you see her." As the days, months, and years went by, I didn't have to consciously consider this as much. I just naturally responded this way. Intentions are powerful. One other recommendation is to journal and reflect on your intentions. Remember the previous chapter on reflection. You might find that writing down your ideas and goals, backed up with daily intentions, makes the idea more real and makes you accountable to the most important leader in your world, you. Remember, it starts with you.

Do What's Right, Every Time

When I worked for Celeste in the predominantly Human-Centered Leadership organization, we had a chief medical officer, Dr. Mishra, whose hallmark answer to any issue or conflict was, "Well, we need to do the right thing." The answer was always pretty simple. We do what's right for the patient, for the families, for the team member, or for the community. Dr. Mishra was a living legend and was revered by everyone from the NICU nurses to the ED doctors to the rehabilitation care technicians to the plant facilities crew. Everyone knew how Dr. Mishra rolled, and he rarely lost in a conflict. I consider it an honor to watch effective healthcare leaders like Dr. Mishra navigate their way through a world focused on metrics and money while meeting the aim to also provide safe and quality care to human beings. It really is a complex world we live in, but if we simplify our "why," we will find that the answer is generally to do what's right. As we recall our critical care director, Robert, who advocated a shift to open visitation in the ICU, he appealed to the nurses' sense of fidelity. Fidelity means that nurses are faithful to the promises they make as professionals to provide quality and compassionate care to their patients (ANA, 2015). Fidelity aligns with the basic approach to always do what's right. When faced with a leader or colleague who is interrupting your joy, pause, speak calmly, and do what's right.

Zero-Sum Game

To summarize the influence of "joy interrupters" in our human-centered world, let's visit the concept of *zero-sum game* versus *non-zero-sum game*. These are notions used in game and economic theory as well as politics but really apply to leadership in healthcare as well. In fact, some might call healthcare leadership a game! When we take part in a *zero-sum game*, the "players" are competitive, and as one person gains momentum or success, others lose in some way. Remember Unma? When I was successful, Unma felt that I was taking something away from her. I was somehow diminishing her success, and she let me know. Have you ever worked with a leader who protected their knowledge or tools to the extent that others failed? Another example comes to mind with regard to the ICU's receipt of the Beacon Award. A Beacon Award signifies an ICU's positive and supportive work environment with an equal focus on using evidence-based information to improve patient outcomes (AACN, 2020). The awarded ICU was just one of many critical care units within a large health system comprised of eight hospitals. The whole hospital system celebrated the success of this team with much fanfare, however, when asked to share their best practices and documents with other critical care units in sister hospitals, the nurse manager and director of that ICU refused, citing confidential information, and executive leaders supported their stance. There was nothing proprietary about their success. Why were they protecting their success rather than sharing it? Did they fear the success of others might diminish their own? Information that could have ultimately improved patient care, outcomes, and nursing work environments was kept "secret." Imagine the joy and success that could have been shared.

On the other hand, a *non-zero-sum game* describes the dynamics of a leadership team that isn't strictly competitive. *Non-zero sum* means one leader's gain is a potential win for other leaders. For example, when one medical-surgical unit is knocking it out of the park with patient experience scores, they not only share what they're doing, they mentor others to strive for the same outcomes. Human-Centered Leaders play a *non-zero-sum* game. We aim to recognize and celebrate collective wins through the shared vision for optimal patient outcomes. As individuals and teams gain momentum and add to our "win" column, the entire system benefits.

Joy interrupters and *zero-sum* gamers should be an expectation in our Human-Centered Leadership lives. Healthcare is, in fact, a reflection of the world. With reality in check, we can't expect rainbows and unicorns, rather we embrace the full spectrum of diverse personalities, styles, and human ways of being. Of prime importance is that we, as Human-Centered Leaders, recognize we can't change others; we have to change ourselves. Remember all the ground we covered on self-awareness and mindfulness? If we learn to control our responses to joy interrupters with patience, kindness, evidence, intention, and aiming to do what's right, everyone wins, particularly our patients.

DISCUSSION QUESTIONS

1. Consider a recent crucial conversation with a colleague who interrupted your joy. How did you respond? What was good about it, and what techniques described in this chapter could you have used?

2. Think of an example of a *zero-sum game* experience in your past or current work. Think of a *non-zero-sum game* experience and share.

3. Think about a leader in your organization or school who brings joy to your day, rather than interrupting it. What does that leader do to bring joy?

REFLECTION

Exercise your brain's "intention muscle" by practicing. Read the following three sentences to yourself and pay attention to how each simple change in language creates a different expectation for the experience.

"I **hope** to enjoy today's staff meeting."

Notice how you actually think about this—your internal pictures, voices, and feelings, and note them here.

_____

_____

"I **want** to enjoy today's staff meeting."

Notice how you actually think about this—your internal pictures, voices, and feelings—what is **different from the first statement?**

_____

_____

"I **intend** to enjoy today's staff meeting."

Notice how you actually think about this—your internal pictures, voices, and feelings—what is **different from the first two statements?**

_____

_____

REFERENCES

American Association of Critical Care Nurses. (2020). *Beacon Award: Be a beacon of excellence for your community, hospital, and patients.* https://www.aacn.org/nursing-excellence/beacon-awards

American Nurses Association. (2015). *Code of ethics for nurses with interpretive statements.* https://www.nursingworld.org/practice-policy/nursing-excellence/ethics/code-of-ethics-for-nurses/

Bradberry, T. & Greaves, J. (2009). *Emotional intelligence 2.0.* TalentSmart.

Hallbom, T., & Hallbom, K. (2000). *The intent setting process*. https://www.nlpca.com/articles/Bringforthism-and-the-art-of-creating-your-ideal-future-by-kris-hallbom.html

Patterson, K., Grenny, J., McMillan, R., & Switzler, A. (2012). *Crucial conversations: Tools for talking when the stakes are high*. McGraw-Hill.

Ricciardi, R. (2019). *2019-2021 Presidential Call to Action: Infuse Joy*. Sigma. https://www.sigmanursing.org/why-sigma/organizational-leadership/presidential-call-to-action-2019-2021

RECOMMENDED READING

Achor, S. (2018). *Big potential: How transforming the pursuit of success raises our achievement, happiness, and well-being*. Penguin Random House.

Achor, S. (2010). *The happiness advantage: How a positive brain fuels success in work and life*. Penguin Random House.

Becker, S., & Gamble, M. (2018). *Healthcare as a zero-sum game: 7 key points*. Becker's Hospital Review. https://www.beckershospitalreview.com/hospital-management-administration/healthcare-as-a-zero-sum-game-7-key-points.html

Nowack, K. (2017). Facilitating successful behavior change: Beyond goal setting to goal flourishing. *Consulting Psychology Journal: Practice and Research*, 69(3), 153–171. http://dx.doi.org/10.1037/cpb0000088

Ovul, S., Zhang, T., Gino, F., & Bazerman, M. H. (2016). Overcoming the outcome bias: Making intentions matter. Organizational Behavior and Human Decision Processes, 137, 13–26.

PART V
JOIN THE MOVEMENT

Human-Centered Leadership is more than learned skills. It's a philosophy, a practice, a way of life, and a movement that is especially pertinent to the profession of nursing and the industry of healthcare. Let's look at ways we can all contribute to the momentum and movement of Human-Centered Leadership.

Chapter 16

Imagine What Could Be...

"The only real difference between evolution and revolution is the pace of change."
—**Tim Porter-O'Grady and Kathy Malloch** (2018, p. 505),
Nurse Leaders, Researchers, and Authors

E volution refers to the gradual development of changes in something or someone over time. There are periods of energy bursts along with quiet during evolution that allow change to settle and become sustainable. That's how growth in a profession, an organization, or even a human occurs. Within evolution there also exists revolution. A revolution occurs when a fundamental change in the way of thinking about or visualizing something occurs. A revolution is a paradigm shift. The evolution of nursing leadership, since the inception of nursing in the 1880s has included periods of what some might call "flavor of the month," approaches to leadership. Over time we've seen the momentum of traditional leadership styles shift to servant to transformational to authentic and so on. So, what makes Human-Centered Leadership different? The Human-Centered Leader isn't an approach with mutually exclusive ways of being or singular constructs to guide behaviors. Rather, Human-Centered Leadership is a holistic leadership approach and theory that includes a missing player in all the other theories: the leader. Starting with self is a key difference in which the leader prioritizes self-care, self-compassion, self-awareness, and mindfulness. The leader can then emanate the same care for self, outward to teams and patients. We believe Human-Centered Leadership is not another "flavor of the month," rather, it's an evidence-based leadership style rooted in the essence and history of nursing. It's more than a style or an approach; it's who you, as a leader, choose to be. It's not a destination; it's a practice. It is, in fact, a revolution within the history of nursing's evolution as a profession. We believe Human-Centered Leadership has always been in our midst. It's only now that we have named it. A revolution requires a critical mass of recognition and engagement. As more individuals shift their paradigm, the collective tipping point of the revolution transforms to become a natural part of the growth or evolution of a profession. The way of being becomes sustained and stands the test of time. Being part of a revolution is innovative and requires courage. History documents revolutions through the social maturation and publication of how people, process, and outcomes evolve over long spans of time. We hope you'll join us with even a small contribution to this revolution of evidence-based nursing leadership. As with any complex system, the smallest efforts result in big changes.

Butterflies, Chaos, and Your Part in All This

Most of us have heard the concept of the butterfly effect and the question posed by MIT scientist, Edward Lorenz in 1969: "Does the flap of a butterfly's wings in Brazil set off a tornado in Texas?" Lorenz was using a metaphor to illustrate the idea that complex systems, like the weather, exhibit unpredictable behaviors and outcomes when there are small variances or changes in the initial conditions. In the case of the butterfly, the flapping of the wings sets off a cascade of small yet exponentially influential responses in weather variables that produces the tornado in Texas. Sounds dramatic but remember, this is a metaphor to show us how minor or seemingly insignificant changes in smaller environments can cause big change in the larger system. Lorenz's foundational concepts became what we know as chaos theory. How do the butterfly effect and chaos connect to a nursing leadership theory? As mentioned previously in Part III, we believe

Human-Centered Leadership and consistent application of the attributes of the Awakener, the Connector, and the Upholder in everyday leadership from the bedside to the boardroom will result in incremental and significant change in the "outer circle" metrics of an organization: a culture of excellence, trust, and caring. Recall the discussion around change in Part IV. Chaos or, as is the case in healthcare, the unpredictability of humans, is really the edge of change. Chaos is the space where, you, as a nurse leader, get to choose how to react and adapt. You get the choice of resisting chaos and change or welcoming it with a mindful and authentic presence. As a Human-Centered Leader, you choose the latter and pave a new way not just for the individual or the unit but for the entire system or organization. For example, as a nurse manager, when faced with implementing a new hospital-wide mandated hourly rounding procedure, you recognize your rehabilitation unit is unique in its staffing ratios, patient population, and care delivery model. You can force the model to fit your unit, or you can choose to advocate for small changes based on your knowledge and input from the bedside nurses. The small choices and changes you make will influence outcomes from patient satisfaction to nurse satisfaction to safety and quality. Not every innovation requires a patent. Often, it's the small innovations that add up. Be a butterfly and watch as you and your teams gain momentum in not just meeting, but exceeding goals.

To learn more on how to be part of the Human-Centered Leadership movement, please visit our website: www.uleadership.com. Also, consider testing the theory against journey to excellence metrics. We would love to partner with you in this revolution.

Momentum

According to Adam Braun (2014), American entrepreneur, author, and philanthropist, for any movement to gain momentum, it must start with a small action. Braun's story is a living example of momentum and, we would venture to say, the butterfly effect. While in college, Braun took part in a study abroad and was able to visit many countries. In each country, he would ask local children what they wanted most in the world. In India, a young boy begging on the streets told Braun what he wanted most was a pencil. Braun gave the boy his pencil, and the inspiration for Pencils of Promise, a non-profit organization that builds schools and increases educational opportunities in the developing world was born. Braun recounts:

I reached into my backpack, handed him my pencil, and watched as a wave of possibility washed over him. A smile erupted and his eyes brightened. And I saw then, the profound power and promise brought through something as small as giving a pencil to just one child. (p. 35)

As of 2020, Braun's organization has founded more than 500 schools and served more than 100,000 children throughout the developing world including Ghana, Guatemala, Laos, and Nicaragua.

We want to challenge each of you to consider how you can give the proverbial pencil to a child and be part of a revolution in healthcare to shift the tide from numbers-focused back to a human-centered approach. We fully recognize the need to be profitable and to meet metrics that keep hospitals and healthcare organizations in business. We also unequivocally believe a human-centered approach to leading in healthcare will organically produce the much sought-after financial and quality metrics. The "ask" is to simply embrace and live the attributes of the Awakener, the Connector, and the Upholder. Do you have to go out tomorrow and make a lot of changes in your life? No. We believe if you focus on recognizing the humanity in yourself and in others as a starting point, you will be making a significant difference in the lives of those entrusted to your care. If each of the four million nurses just in the United States embraced this concept, can you imagine the impact we would have on the world?

Don't Let Anything or Anyone Stop You

Many of you probably identified with a number of the attributes of the Awakener, the Connector, and the Upholder. You may have even said, "I already do most of this." Hopefully, there were also many of you who recognized the missing link in your human-centered world, which might have been "you." Our story, which we shared in the preface, might have sounded familiar and may be much like your story. We were successful in leading teams to industry leading quality, patient, workforce, and financial metrics. We served our nurses and helped them grow. We changed cultures. We also forgot ourselves in the mix. We "served" our way into burnout, and we realized our well-being was at risk. Luckily, we found our tribe, and we discovered the key to leading in healthcare is to truly start with self. We've all heard, "You need to take care of *you* before you can take care of others." We now realize how exceptionally important this is for the sustainability of Human-Centered Leaders.

DISCUSSION QUESTIONS

1. How will you put Human-Centered Leadership into action? Today? Tomorrow? Over the next few months?
2. Share some real-world ways you can lead the quiet revolution in your unit or in your world.

REFLECTION

As you consider the butterfly effect and the concept that small changes at a local level influence outcomes at a higher level, how have you "flapped your wings" in the past? How will you take flight at work and at home?

_____

_____

_____

_____

_____

_____

REFERENCES

Braun, A. (2014). *The promise of a pencil: How an ordinary person can create extraordinary change.* Scribner.

Lorenz, E. (1969). Atmospheric predictability as revealed by naturally occurring analogues. *Journal of Atmospheric Sciences*, 26(4), 636-646. https://doi.org/10.1175%2F1520-0469%281969%2926%3C636%3AAPARBN%3E2.0.CO%3B2

RECOMMENDED READING

Vernon, J. Understanding the butterfly effect. *American Scientist*, 105(3). https://doi.org/10.1511/2017.105.3.130

About the Authors

Kay Kennedy, Susan Campis, Lucy Leclerc

Dr. Kay Kennedy is a nurse executive, nurse educator, and entrepreneur. By combining a love for nurses, patients, and quality improvement, she has led large nursing teams to create healthy work environments, satisfied patients, and consistent, high-quality care. Dr. Kennedy has held multiple leadership roles, from the bedside to Chief Nursing Officer. Dr. Kennedy's goal as a leader is to ignite innovative problem-solving, develop others to be their best, and lead by serving others.

Dr. Lucy Leclerc is a nurse executive, entrepreneur, and Assistant Professor of Nursing at Kennesaw State University, where she teaches leadership, professionalism, and ethics to the future of nursing. Lucy's research focuses on nursing leadership in practice and in academia. She serves on the editorial board of the *Journal of Nursing Education* and has published research in many peer-reviewed journals. Dr. Leclerc seeks to reveal what already exists within nurses and nursing teams…excellence and professionalism.

Susan Campis, MSN, RN, CCRN-K, NE-BC has served in progressive leadership roles for over 12 years, her last role being Executive Director of the Grady Burn Center at Grady Hospital in Atlanta, Georgia. Susan is a nurse leader whose passion for coaching and mentoring helped produce successful nursing teams and metrics throughout her career. She works to create a safe and healthy work culture where her team can be and perform at their best, ensuring quality care, safety, and positive human experiences.

Appendix A

Human-Centered Leadership in Healthcare Appraisal: Do a Pulse Check

Instructions: Listed below are 15 statements. Each statement provides a possible strategy for leadership. Rate each statement on a scale of 1 to 5, indicating how likely you are to use this strategy. Don't answer as you think you should, answer as you actually conduct yourself.

1=Rarely, if ever   2=Not very often   3=Sometimes   4=Very Often   5=Always

Score		Statements
	a.	I provide a safe environment for my team members to grow and expect accountability for individual growth plans.
	b.	I practice self-care, self-compassion, and self-awareness as a role model for my team.
	c.	I make sure my team members are plugged into processes and structures (councils and committees) to support the emergence of new ideas.
	d.	I facilitate and support structures and processes (councils and committees) so innovation can emerge from my team at the point of care or work.
	e.	I use self-reflection to recognize humanity in myself and my team members.
	f.	I embrace unpredictability and change as the norm by endorsing experimentation of ideas to generate innovation.
	g.	I provide honest feedback and address team member behaviors that are inconsistent with a culture of excellence.

	h.	I support my team with respect, kindness, empathy, and empowerment.
	i.	I unify my team and others around a shared vision and mission.
	j.	I ensure resources are available for my team to do research and adopt evidence-based practice.
	k.	I lead my team with an open mind to respect everyone and withhold judgment.
	l.	I aim to build mutual respect and trust through nurturing intentional connections with others.
	m.	I establish a learning culture with high expectations for ongoing learning and growth.
	n.	I focus my attention, awareness, and energy on the present moment when with my team members.
	o.	I support, recognize, and appreciate independent problem-solving and individual contributions at the point of service.

Scoring: The 15 statements you just read are listed below under three (3) categories. Each category contains the letters of five (5) statements. Record the number you rated for each statement. Calculate the total for each category.

Concentration						Total
Awakener	a.	d.	g.	j.	m.	
Connect	c.	f.	i.	l.	o.	
Uphold	b.	e.	h.	k.	n.	

Results:

My primary focus as a Human-Centered Leader is being a/an _____(Your HIGHEST score)

My complementary areas of focus as a Human-Centered Leader are

_____ (SECOND highest score)

_____ (THIRD highest score)

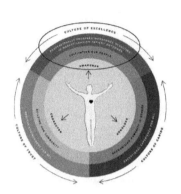

Awakener

- *Fundamental premise:* Cultivating people leads to a Culture of Excellence

- *Strategic philosophy:* By revealing the potential excellence in each of your team members, you awaken what already exists, i.e., innovation, propensity for teaching and learning, etc. This leads to a professionally prepared workforce which results in market-leading patient outcomes.

- *Attributes:*
  - Motivator
  - Coach
  - Mentor
  - Architect
  - Advocate

- *Ways to strengthen the Awakener:*
  - Learn more about coaching. Rose Sherman's book, *The Nurse Leader Coach* is a great resource with real-world examples of how to coach from a human-centered perspective.
  - Motivation is vital to helping develop your team members. Daniel Pink's book *Drive: The Surprising Truth About What Motivates* helps the Human-Centered Leader zero in on *intrinsic* motivation, which is what drives all of us to grow and learn.
  - Pay close attention to Chapter 7, which highlights the attributes of the Awakener in action.

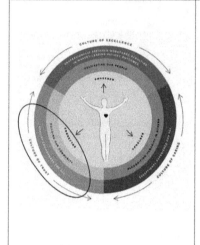

Connector

- *Fundamental premise:* Building community leads to a Culture of Trust

- *Strategic philosophy:* By engineering visible and invisible architecture for voice, connection, and change, you construct healthy work environments for all team members at all levels.

- *Attributes:*
  o Collaborator
  o Supporter
  o Edgewalker
  o Engineer
  o Authentic Communicator

- *Ways to strengthen the Connector in me:*
  o Become familiar with AACN Healthy Work Environment guidelines.
  o Study professional governance and structural empowerment. ANCC Magnet resources are a good place to start.
  o Practice active listening to enhance authentic communication.
  o Pay close attention to Chapter 8, which highlights the attributes of the Connector in action.

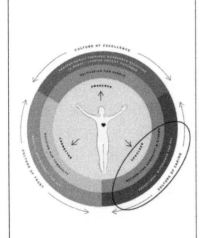

Upholder

- *Fundamental premise:* Recognizing humanity in others leads to a Culture of Caring

- *Strategic philosophy:* By embracing and acknowledging humanity in self and in others through authentic presence, emotional intelligence, self-care, and mindfulness, you craft an environment that leads to an exceptional experience for all team members at all levels. As team members feel cared for, they will, in turn, care the same way for their patients.

- *Attributes:*
  - Mindful
  - Others-Oriented
  - Emotionally Aware
  - Socially and Organizationally Aware
  - Personally Well and Healthy

- *Way to strengthen the Upholder in me:*
  - Study emotional intelligence and determine areas I need to focus on for growth.
  - Develop an individual self-care plan
  - Engage in reflective journaling in *Shifts*
  - Study empathy and vulnerability: Brené Brown is an expert to follow.
  - Pay close attention to Chapter 9, which highlights the attributes of the Upholder in action.

Appendix B

Human-Centered Leadership Dimensions and Attributes with Definitions

Awakener	Cultivates our people
Motivator	Establishes a learning culture with high expectations for ongoing learning for self and others
Coach	Provides honest feedback, address behaviors inconsistent with learning culture
Mentor	Advises on member accountability for individual growth plans
Architect	Designs structures/processes so innovation can emerge
Advocate	Ensures resources are available for best practice and professional growth
Connector	Builds our community
Collaborator	Unifies others around shared mission and vision
Supporter	Supports, recognizes, and appreciates independent problem-solving and individual contributions at the point of service
Edgewalker	Embraces change/chaos by endorsing experimentation of ideas to generate innovation
Engineer	Ensures people are plugged into processes/structures for emergence of new ideas
Authentic Communicator	Builds mutual respect and trust through nurturing intentional connections with others
Upholder	Recognizes humanity in others
Mindful	Focuses attention, awareness, and energy on present
Others Oriented	Supports with respect, kindness, empathy, and empowerment

Emotionally Aware	Recognizes and embraces humanity at all levels; self-reflective
Socially and Organizationally Aware	Leads with an open mind
Personally Well and Healthy	Practices self-care, self-compassion, self-awareness

Note: From Leclerc, L., Kennedy, K., & Campis, S. (2020). Human-centered leadership in healthcare: An idea that's time has come. *Nursing Administration Quarterly*, *44*(2), 117-126 and Leclerc, L., Kennedy, K., & Campis, S. (2021). Human-centered leadership in healthcare: A contemporary nursing leadership theory generated via constructivist grounded theory. *Journal of Nursing Management*, 29, 294-306

Appendix C

Crosswalk of ANCC (2015) Magnet Standards with Human-Centered Leadership Dimensions and Outcomes

Magnet Outcome Requirement	Human-Centered Leadership Dimension	Expected Culture Change
Commitment to Culture of Safety	Awakener	Culture of Excellence
Mentoring plans	Awakener	Culture of Excellence
Improve nursing practice environment	Connector	Culture of Trust
RN satisfaction: Leadership access and responsiveness	Upholder	Culture of Caring
Nurse involvement in population heath outreach	Connector	Culture of Trust
Delivery of culturally and socially sensitive care	Connector	Culture of Trust
Nurses and interprofessional groups contribute to strategic goals of organization	Connector	Culture of Trust
RN satisfaction: Autonomy; Interprofessional relationships; Fundamentals of quality; Adequacy of resources and staffing	Upholder	Culture of Caring

RN-to-RN teamwork and collaboration / interprofessional collaboration	Connector	Culture of Trust
Decrease in never events/quality improvement based on EBP	Awakener	Culture of Excellence
Advancement of research in nursing/ interprofessional	Connector/Awakener	Culture of Trust Culture of Excellence
Decrease in turnover rate	Upholder	Culture of Caring
Improved patient experience	Upholder	Culture of Caring
Improvements based on patient feedback and service recovery	Upholder	Culture of Caring
Increasing percentage of nurses certified in their specialty	Awakener	Culture of Excellence
Increasing percentage of nurses with BSN degree	Awakener	Culture of Excellence
Improve patient outcomes secondary to nurses' participation in professional development activities	Awakener	Culture of Excellence
Effective transition to new roles	Awakener	Culture of Excellence
Individualized professional development plans for nurses at all levels, based on performance review, etc.	Awakener	Culture of Excellence

Note: From Leclerc, L., Kennedy, K., & Campis, S. (2021). Human-centered leadership in healthcare: A contemporary nursing leadership theory generated via constructivist grounded theory. *Journal of Nursing Management*, 00, 1–1.
For ANCC Magnet Standards see American Nurses Credentialing Center (2015). ANCC Magnet Recognition Program. https://www.nursingworld.org/organizational-programs/magnet/

Appendix D

Crosswalk of American Nurses Association Code of Ethics for Nurses (2015) with Supporting Culture Created by Human-Centered Leaders

ANA COE Provision	Description	Human-Centered Leadership Dimension	Associated Culture
Provision 1	The nurse practices with compassion and respect for the inherent dignity, worth, and unique attributes of every person.	Upholder	Culture of Caring
Provision 2	The nurse's primary commitment is to the patient, whether an individual, family, group, community, or population.	Upholder	Culture of Caring
Provision 3	The nurse promotes, advocates for, and protects the rights, health, and safety of the patient.	Upholder	Culture of Caring
Provision 4	The nurse has authority, accountability, and responsibility for nursing practice; makes decisions; and takes action consistent with the obligation to provide optimal patient care	Awakener	Culture of Excellence

Provision 5	The nurse owes the same duties to self as to others, including the responsibility to promote health and safety, preserve wholeness of character and integrity, maintain competence, and continue personal and professional growth.	Upholder	Culture of Caring
Provision 6	The nurse, through individual and collective effort, establishes, maintains, and improves the ethical environment of the work setting and conditions of employment that are conducive to safe, quality healthcare.	Connector	Culture of Trust
Provision 7	The nurse, in all roles and settings, advances the profession through research and scholarly inquiry, professional standards development, and the generation of both nursing and health policy.	Awakener	Culture of Excellence
Provision 8	The nurse collaborates with other health professionals and the public to protect human rights, promote health diplomacy, and reduce health disparities.	Connector	Culture of Trust
Provision 9	The profession of nursing, collectively through its professional organizations, must articulate nursing values, maintain the integrity of the profession, and integrate principles of social justice into nursing and health policy.	Connector	Culture of Trust

Note: For ANA COE provisions see American Nurses Association. (2015). *Code of ethics with interpretative statements.* http:// www.nursingworld.org/MainMenuCategories/EthicsStandards/ CodeofEthicsforNurses/Code-ofEthics-For-Nurses.htm

Appendix E

Crosswalk of AACN Draft Essentials for BSN, MSN, and DNP Programs with Human-Centered Leadership Dimensions, Attributes, and Outcomes

DRAFT Essentials Domains, Descriptors, Contextual Statements, and Competencies May 2020
Domain 10: Personal, Professional, and Leadership Development

Descriptor: Participation in activities and self-reflection that foster personal health, resilience, and well-being, lifelong learning, and support the acquisition of nursing expertise and assertion of leadership.

Contextual Statement: Competency in Personal, Professional, and Leadership Development encompasses three areas: 1) development of the nurse as an individual, resilient, agile, and capable of adapting to ambiguity and change; 2) development of the nurse as a professional, responsible, and accountable for lifelong learning and ongoing self-reflection; and 3) development of the nurse as a leader, proficient in asserting control, influence, and power in professional and personal contexts. Development of these dimensions requires a commitment to personal growth, sustained expansion of professional knowledge and expertise, and determined leadership practice in a variety of contexts is required.

Graduates must develop attributes and skills critical to the viability of the profession and practice environments. The aim is to promote diversity and retention in the profession, avoidance of stress-induced emotional and mental exhaustion, and re-direction of energy from negative perceptions to positive influence through leadership opportunities.

Competencies:

10.1 Demonstrate a commitment to personal health and well-being.

10.2 Demonstrate a spirit of inquiry that fosters flexibility and professional maturity.

10.3 Develop capacity for leadership.

	Description	Human-Centered Leadership: Book Chapter	Dimension	Attribute	Outcome
10.1	Demonstrate a commitment to personal health and well-being.	**Chapter 3:** The Human at the Center **Chapter 4:** Self-Care and Self-Compassion **Chapter 5:** Mindfulness **Chapter 9:** The Upholder	Upholder	Personally well & healthy, Mindful	Culture of Caring
10.2	Demonstrate a spirit of inquiry that fosters flexibility and professional maturity.	**Chapter 5:** Mindfulness **Chapter 7:** The Awakener **Chapter 10:** Emotional Intelligence **Chapter 12:** The Three Cs: Competence, Capability, and Complexity **Chapter 13:** Reflective Practice **Chapter 14:** Innovation	Awakener	Motivator	Culture of Excellence

| 10.3 | Develop capacity for leadership. | **Chapter 6**: It's not about you **Chapter 7**: The Awakener **Chapter 8**: The Connector **Chapter 9**: The Upholder | Awakener Connector Upholder | Motivator, Coach, Mentor, Advocate, Architect Supporter, Collaborator, Edgewalker, Engineer, Authentic Communicator Personally well & healthy, Emotional Awareness, Others-oriented, Social and Organizational Awareness, Mindful | Culture of Excellence Culture of Trust Culture of Caring |

Note: For AACN Draft Essentials see American Association of Colleges of Nursing. (2020). *DRAFT Essentials Domains, Descriptors, Contextual Statements, and Competencies.* https://www.aacnnursing.org/About-AACN/AACN-Governance/Committees-and-Task-Forces/Essentials

American Association of Critical Care Nurses (2016) Healthy Work Environment (HWE) Crosswalk with Human-Centered Leadership (HCL) Dimensions and Cultures

HWE Standard	HWE Questions	Human-Centered Leadership Dimension	Human-Centered Leadership Culture
Skilled Communication	Administrators, nurse managers, physicians, nurses and other staff maintain frequent communication to prevent each other from being surprised or caught off guard by decisions.	Awakener Connector Upholder	Excellence Trust Caring
	Administrators, nurse managers, physicians, nurses and other staff make sure their actions match their words- they "walk their talk."	Awakener Connector Upholder	Excellence Trust Caring
	Administrators, nurse managers, physicians, nurses and other staff have zero-tolerance for disrespect and abuse. If they see or hear someone being disrespectful, they hold them accountable regardless of the person's role or position	Awakener Connector Upholder	Excellence Trust Caring

True Collaboration	Administrators, nurse managers, and physicians involve nurses and other staff to an appropriate degree when making decisions	Collaborator	Trust
	Nurses and other staff feel able to influence the policies, procedures, and bureaucracy around them	Connector	Trust
	When administrators, nurse managers, and physicians speak with nurses and other staff, it's not one-way communication or order giving. Instead they seek input and use it to shape decisions	Connector Upholder	Trust Caring
Effective Decision Making	Administrators, nurse managers, physicians, nurses and other staff are consistent in their use of data-driven, logical decision-making processes to make sure their decisions are the highest quality	Awakener Collaborator	Excellence Trust
	The right departments, professions, and groups are involved in important decisions	Collaborator	Trust
	Administrators, nurse managers, physicians, nurses and other staff are careful to consider the patient's and family's perspectives whenever they are making important decisions.	Upholder	Caring

Appropriate Staffing	Administrators and nurse managers work with nurses and other staff to make sure there are enough staff to maintain patient safety	Collaborator	Trust
	Administrators and nurse managers make sure there is the rights mix of nurses and other staff to ensure optimal outcomes	Awakener	Excellence
	Support services are provided at a level that allows nurses and other staff to spend their time on the priorities and requirements of patient and family care	Upholder	Caring
Meaningful Recognition	The formal reward and recognition systems work to make nurses and other staff feel valued	Upholder	Caring
	Administrators, nurse managers, physicians, nurses and other staff members speak up and let people know when they have done a good job	Upholder	Caring
	There are motivating opportunities for personal growth, development and advancement	Awakener	Excellence

Authentic Leadership	Most nurses and other staff here have a positive relationship with their nurse leaders	Upholder	Caring
	Nurse leaders demonstrate an understanding of the requirements and dynamics at the point of care and use this knowledge to work for a healthy work environment.	Awakener	Excellence
	Nurse leaders are given the access and authority required to play a role in making key decisions	Collaborator	Trust

Note: For ANCC HWE Standards see American Association of Critical Care Nurses (AACN) (2016). *AACN Standards for Establishing and Sustaining Healthy Work Environments: Journey to Excellence*, 2nd ed. American Association of Critical Care Nurses.

A free ebook edition is available with the purchase of this book.

To claim your free ebook edition:

Visit MorganJamesBOGO.com
Sign your name CLEARLY in the space
Complete the form and submit a photo of
the entire copyright page
You or your friend can download the ebook
to your preferred device

Morgan James
BOGO™

A **FREE** ebook edition is available for you
or a friend with the purchase of this print book.

CLEARLY SIGN YOUR NAME ABOVE

Instructions to claim your free ebook edition:
1. Visit MorganJamesBOGO.com
2. Sign your name CLEARLY in the space above
3. Complete the form and submit a photo
   of this entire page
4. You or your friend can download the ebook
   to your preferred device

Print & Digital Together Forever.

Snap a photo   Free ebook   Read anywhere

Printed in the USA
CPSIA information can be obtained
at www.ICGtesting.com
LVHW041211210924
791747LV00002B/119